ABSOLUTELY
THE WORDS

BⓀXTREE

in association with
Channel Four Television
Company Limited

First published in the UK in 1992 by
BOXTREE LIMITED, Broadwall House,
21 Broadwall, London SE1 9PL

10987654321

Text Copyright © Absolutely Productions Ltd., 1992

Designed by Design 23

Printed and bound in Great Britain
by Cox and Wyman Ltd., Reading, Berkshire

A catalogue record for this book is available from the
British Library.

ISBN 1 85283 787 X

"ABSOLUTELY"
is written and performed by:

Pete Baikie
Morwenna Banks
Jack Docherty
Moray Hunter
Gordon Kennedy
John Sparkes

These scripts were selected for this
compendium by the cast from the first
three series of "Absolutely", and were
edited by Alan Nixon.

"ABSOLUTELY"
is produced for Channel Four Television
by Absolutely Productions Ltd.

FOREWORD
by our Lord the Jesus Christ

Hi there!

You can imagine how surprised I was to be sent a copy of this book and asked to write a foreword for it, especially considering that the postal service up here is useless (Saint Paul still hasn't had one reply from those bloody Corinthians), and I've been dead for nigh on 2000 years.

Happily this didn't ruin my enjoyment of this excellent compilation of sketches by my favourite apostles of comedy. OK, sometimes they take the piss, but you learn to be thick-skinned in this game; we've all got our crosses to bear.

No question, it's a blinding good read. Quite frankly, I haven't laughed so much since we all scarpered and left Judas to pick up the tab at the Last Supper.

Being a showbiz family ourselves, we watch the show religiously, although my father says he's seen it all before.

Many people say that the television sketch show is out of date, but then they say that about me. Sometimes the natural lifespan of an idea is only three minutes. A miracle is a good example of this. Remember when I turned the trousers into bread? Two minutes 45. The perfect lengthfor a metaphysical phenomenon. Always leave them wanting...

Or, as "Ha" the Egyptian God of Amusing

things put it, when he popped over to borrow my new Lenny Bruce tapes, " ⌐⊸ ⫯⊹ ↘⌐ ∩|⪡ ⊸⊠ ⩙!". A good point well made.

Enjoy the book.

Your sincerely,

J.C.

P.S. Watch out for a plague of slippers Chistmas time.

· AN ABSOLUTELY SKETCH ·

NOT QUITE THE FOREWORD

Dear Reader,

Good luck in the future.

Best wishes,

The Absolutelies

"ABSOLUTELY" - Series One

Transmission: 23rd May - 27th June 1989

The Nice Family - Kitchen
Dial-A-Pizza
Don & George - Cantankerous
Denzil - Table
Calum - Living Room
Little Girl - Queen
The Nice Family - Points of View
Foot and Ear
Denzil - Shelves
SJFA Cup Draw
Little Girl - Baby Jesus
Don & George - Bargains
The Nice Family - Postie

Designer: Margaret Howat
Director: Phil Chilvers
Producer: Alan Nixon

THE NICE FAMILY - Kitchen

THE NICE FAMILY KITCHEN. FATHER IS SITTING AT THE BREAKFAST TABLE. HE IS WEARING A NEAT FAWN-PULLOVER-AND-BROWN-SLACKS COMBINATION. HE PERUSES HIS NEWSPAPER, "THE DAILY SENSIBLE", WHOSE MAIN HEADLINE INFORMS - "Tidy Man Gets Top Job". MOTHER, AT THE SINK, HAS HER BACK TO THE CAMERA. AS SHE WASHES THE DISHES, SHE HUMS IN A SEMI-MUSICAL FASHION. FATHER NOTES AN ADVERTISEMENT IN HIS PAPER.

FATHER
Well, my wife and mother of my family, I must say that small, snug-fitting, battery-operated hearing-aid must greatly assist those unfortunate enough to suffer from hearing difficulties.

**HE FURIOUSLY LICKS HIS THUMB
BEFORE TURNING THE PAGE. ELDEST
SON ENTERS. HE IS DRESSED
IDENTICALLY TO FATHER.**

ELDEST SON
Morning, father.

FATHER
Good morning, eldest son.

THEY SHAKE HANDS

ELDEST SON
Good morning, mother.

**MOTHER GIVES A RUBBER GLOVE-CLAD
WAVE.**

ELDEST SON
Have you enough dishes, mother?

**MOTHER GIVES AN EMPHATIC THUMBS-
UP. ELDEST SON JOINS HIS FATHER AT
THE BREAKFAST TABLE.**

ELDEST SON
Ah, breakfast! The most important
breakfast of the day.

**THE DAUGHTER ENTERS. SHE TOO
SPORTS A FAWN SWEATER AND BROWN
SKIRT WHOSE HEM DEMURELY
BRUSHES HER ANKLE SOCKS.**

DAUGHTER
Good morning, father.

FATHER
Good morning, daughter. Well I must say
you're looking very attractive, this
morning. Your sweater is bright, but not
gaudy, and your skirt is business-like but
not frumpy.

DAUGHTER
Thank you for taking the time to mention
it, father.

FATHER
Not at all, daughter.

DAUGHTER
Good morning, mother.

**THIS GETS ANOTHER EXAGGERATED
ACKNOWLEDGEMENT. THE DAUGHTER
SITS DOWN AS THE TWINS, ONE AND
TWO ENTER, DRESSED AS THE OTHERS.**

TWINS 1 & 2
Good morning, family.

ALL
Good morning, twins.

TWIN 2
(SITTING DOWN) Morning, mother.

A BACKWARDS WAVE...

TWIN 1
(GOING TO THE WINDOW)
Morning, mother.

...AND AGAIN

TWIN 1
Well, the weather forecast last night was
very accurate. It is overcast, but it does
seem there is a prospect of brighter
spells later. **(HE JOINS THE OTHERS AT
THE TABLE)**

FATHER
Spoken well, son, spoken well. There are
many occasions when people seem to
find it clever to have a go, as they say,
at the weather forecasters, but in my
opinion they do an extremely difficult job
with great dedication and enthusiasm.
There. That's my opinion on the matter.

**THE FAMILY, HAVING LISTENED
ENRAPTURED, BURST INTO
APPLAUSE.**

FATHER
Well, family, now that we are all here
together, I think it would be an
opportune moment, as they say, to
discuss which television programme each
of us would like to view this evening.

TWIN 2
May I start the discussion off, father?

FATHER
You may, second twin.

TWIN 2
Thank you, father.

THEY SHAKE HANDS.

TWIN 2
I would very much like to view the
wildlife programme with its stunning
photography and its fascinating insight
into a world that we seldom see. I know
for a fact that the subject for this
evening is chimpanzees.

FATHER
Ah yes! The almost human-like behaviour
of the chimpanzee can at times be most
amusing. Now, for my own part, which is
my own, I would very much like to view
the investment programme with its
advice for the small investor.

DAUGHTER
And mother, I know that you expressed
an interest in the Play For Today.

**MOTHER'S HUMMING SQUEAKS IN THE
AFFIRMATIVE AS SHE HOISTS A
THUMBS-UP.**

FATHER
A varied, and yet varied, choice. Ah. It would appear that we have a problem. This evening's drama play and the wildlife are scheduled to be broadcast at one and the same time!

THE FAMILY ARE CRESTFALLEN, MOTHER'S HUMMING NOW DOLOROUS. THERE SEEMS NO SOLUTION TO THIS CALAMITY, UNTIL INSPIRATION LIGHTS UP THE FACE OF ELDEST SON.

ELDEST SON
Wait! I think I may have cracked it. We can use the video recorder to record one programme whilst watching the other, and then - yes, I think this will work - watch the video recording later on.

THE FAMILY JUMPS TO THEIR FEET, CONGRATULATE ELDEST SON, AND SHAKE HIS HAND UNTIL FATHER TAKES CHARGE.

FATHER
Now, now, now. Let us not go overboard, as they say. Back to your seats now. Are you more happy with the situation now, mother?

A HAPPIER HUM AND THUMBS-UP REPLY.

TWIN 1
Oh no!

FATHER
What is up, first twin?

TWIN 1 (DEEPLY CONCERNED)
Can we be sure that the TV drama play is
entirely suitable for family viewing?

FATHER
I'll speak to the authorities directly, on all
our behooves.

**HE GOES TO THE PHONE. AS HE
ADDRESSES THE AUTHORITIES, THE
FAMILY HUDDLE ROUND HIM ANXIOUSLY.**

FATHER
Hello? Is that the authorities? Hello. I'm a
father and I'm phoning on behalf of myself,
a father, and my entire family, who are a
family. I'm seeking your assurance that this
evening's TV drama play is entirely suitable
for family viewing. **(PAUSE)** I see … I see.
Thank you very much, the authorities.

HE TURNS TO THE FAMILY.

FATHER
Family - we're in the clear!

**THEY ALL LEAP IN THE AIR WITH LEVEL-
HEADED JOY.**

DIAL-A-PIZZA

IT'S THAT TIME DURING A PARTY WHEN SOMEONE IS PHONING FOR SOME PIZZAS.

MAN
Hi...yeah...do you deliver pizzas? Great yeah ... Could I have a Napoletana please ... a Quattro Formaggio ... and a Four Seasons ... yeah, and two garlic breads as well, yeah ... and, eh ... could you get one of the pizzas wrong, please? ... any one you want ... doesn't matter ... and, also, the two garlic breads ... just forget them completely ... great, thanks. How long will that be? Forty-five minutes? ... and how long will that actually be? An hour and a half ... lovely, right. So should I phone you back once or twice? Sorry, twice. Right. And the excuses? ... you can't find us, yeah ... and secondly ... we're not in or we're not answering ... and if you don't mind, I'll be quite angry the second time. Sorry, yeah, OK ... **(TO THE PARTY GUESTS)** ... do you want them luke warm?

EVERYONE
No.

MAN
No. Stone cold, please, yeah. Do you want my address? Right, OK ... sure ...

fair enough ... sure.

WOMAN
Doesn't he want the address?

MAN
No, he says he wants to forget and then
phone back.

WOMAN
But he hasn't got your phone number.

MAN
I know ... I'm not very hungry.

DON & GEORGE - Cantankerous

DON AND GEORGE ARE IN A CAGE, SITTING IN RUBBER TYRE-STYLE SWINGS. FOLLOWING A COMMERCIAL BREAK, DON HAS DECIDED TO TRY TO SELL SOME GOODS TO THE VIEWERS HIMSELF.

DON (TO CAMERA)
While we're in a commercial mode, I just thought I'd mention a rather natty pair of plus-threes and an autographed bar of chocolate - £1.50 the pair.

GEORGE
Sorry, Donald, what's going on here?

DON
Just off-loading a couple of items, George.

GEORGE
Well I hardly think this is the time nor the place, Donald, for that sort of thing.

DON
Steady, George. There's no need to be cantankerous.

GEORGE
Oh, cantankerous is it? Oh really?

DON
Yes.
Cantankerous.

GEORGE
I don't think
you even
know what
that means,
Donald.

DON
Yes I do.

GEORGE
I bet you don't.

DON
Well ... I know what some of it means.

GEORGE
What do you mean - you know what
some of it means?

DON
Well, I know what "can't" means.

GEORGE
Yes ...

DON
And I know what the "us" at the end
means.

GEORGE
Yes, but you don't know what the whole
word means.

DON
I can work it out.

GEORGE
How come?

DON
Well, "can't", right, is "unable to".

GEORGE
Yes.

DON
And "us" is "we", "ourselves".

GEORGE
Yes.

DON
So, we're left with "ankero". Can't ankero
us. Unable to ankero we. So all we've got
to do is work out what "ankero" means.

GEORGE
"Cantankerous" is argumentative,
perverse of temper.

DON
Right. So "ankero" must mean "be
pleasant to". Can't ankero us. Unable to be
pleasant to we.

GEORGE
That's not how words are worked out,
Don. Is it?

DON
Of course it is.

GEORGE
OK, OK. If that's how words are worked
out, I'll pick another word, and you tell
me where it came from.

DON
OK. But only if you're going to be
canankerous.

GEORGE
Canankerous?

DON
Yes - <u>able</u> to be pleasant to us.

GEORGE
What do you mean - us? There's only
you.

DON
OK, OK. Can-ankero-me. If you're
canankerome, fair enough.

GEORGE
OK. We'll give it a bash.

DON
Give me a word.

GEORGE
I'll give you a word ... OK ... Restaurant!
Where did that come from?

DON
Restaurant?

GEORGE
Yes. Tell me that, if you're so smart.

DON
Yes ... yes ... **(DESPERATE)** Rest-your-
aunt, it was originally.

GEORGE LOOKS DEEPLY UNIMPRESSED.

DON
Well, people go out walking with their
aunt, they'd get a bit peckish; so they'd
stop off at a Rest-your-aunt for a bite to
eat. Which in time became Restaurant as
we know it.

GEORGE
OK, OK. You've got the "rest", I'll give you
that. And you've got "urant", U-R-A-N-T,
for "your aunt". What about the extra
"a"?

DON
What extra "a"?

GEORGE
R-E-S-T-<u>A</u>-U-R-A-N-T. That 'a'.

DON
Well, obviously ...

GEORGE
Obviously ...?

DON
Originally ... originally ... it was "Rest a)
your aunt", "Rest b) your uncle", "Rest
c) your neice" ... or whatever. But in
time they settled for "Rest a) your aunt"
... restaurant.

GEORGE
So why that one?

DON
Well, it's easy to say.

GEORGE
<u>Resburuncle</u> is not impossible.

DON
OK. Resburuncle is not impossible. But
you try saying "Rest p) your great-great-
grandfather on your mother's side".

**GEORGE (ATTEMPTS TO SAY IT, BUT
GIVES UP)**
I see what you're saying now. I suppose
so, yes.

DENZIL - Table

THE LIVING ROOM OF DENZIL, THE WELSH HOME IMPROVEMENT EXPERT. HE IS SITTING IN AN ARMCHAIR READING A DIY MANUAL. HE NODS AND MUTTERS IN AGREEMENT WITH WHAT HE IS READING, AS IF IT WERE AN ACADEMIC TREATISE.

DENZIL
Oh, yes ... Oh yes. Very good. Very competent. These DIY boys certainly know what they're doing alright.

HE PUTS THE BOOK DOWN ON HIS COFFEE-TABLE - WHICH IMMEDIATELY COLLAPSES. HE OBSERVES THIS, TAKES OUT A NOTEBOOK AND PENCIL, CHECKS THE TIME ON HIS WATCH, AND MAKES A NOTE. GWYNNEDD, DENZIL'S WIFE ENTERS CARRYING A TRAY OF TEA THINGS.

GWYNNEDD
Oh, hello Denzil. I thought you'd mended that table.

DENZIL
I have mended it, Gwynnedd. Somebody have obviously sniffed all the glue out of the leg joint.

GWYNNEDD
Well, don't look at me.

DENZIL
And why shouldn't I look at you? Are
you getting undressed or something?

GWYNNEDD
Don't be so offensive. Anyway, it are
only half past seven.

DENZIL
Half past seven! But that mean it are
eight o'clock!

GWYNNEDD

I didn't know the clock was half an hour
slow.

DENZIL

For heaven's sake, Gwynnedd. It are not
half an hour slow. It are twenty-three
and a half hours fast. Sometimes I think
you have got the brains of a bed-bug.
Where's my coat? I am going to be late
getting down to the Club Sboncyn.

GWYNNEDD

Sboncyn, Sboncyn! It's nothing but
Sboncyn with you these days, isn't it?
When are you going to mend that table?

DENZIL

Gwynnedd, you obviously don't
understand DIY. Preparation is very
important. I will be able to mend the
table ... on Wednesday. After I have
fixed the gas leak in Siencyn's room.

**HE GETS UP TO GET HIS COAT, TAKING
A MUG FROM THE TRAY AS HE DOES
SO. HE TAKES A DRINK AND
IMMEDIATELY SPITS IT OUT.**

DENZIL

What are this filth you have just given
me?

GWYNNEDD
Cheesewater.

DENZIL
Cheesewater! Cheesewater! What are
cheesewater when it are home?

GWYNNEDD
It are a nourishing and soothing cheese
drink. You grate a nice bit of Caerphilly
into a mug and just add boiling water.
Nothing could be easier.

DENZIL
Or more unpleasant.

GWYNNEDD
You should like it then.

DENZIL
That remark are most offensive.

GWYNNEDD
Well, you are most offensive. Why don't
you shove off down the Club Sboncyn
instead of standing here polluting my eyes
with the sight of you?

DENZIL GATHERS UP HIS TOOLS.

DENZIL
I will, I will. I am giving a very important
talk tonight on the subject of everything.
With particular reference to DIY.

GWYNNEDD
Well, I hope Mr Beedeebeedee isn't there.

DENZIL
Any why is that?

GWYNNEDD
Because Mr Beedeebeedee still haven't forgiven you for going round to his house at three o'clock in the morning and putting up shelves in his bedroom.

DENZIL
It needed doing.

GWYNNEDD
And if you do it again, he will call the police.

DENZIL
Mr Beedeebeedee would be a bloody fool if he did that. The police haven't got the first idea about shelving. People just don't appreciate the importance of DIY. Look at Mr Ffiff down the road. He had to go to hospital. There's no need for that. If only he had done his grouting properly he would have been as right as rain. Anyway, I can't stand here talking to you all day - because I can't stand you.

EXITS WITH A SLAM OF THE DOOR.

CALUM - Living Room

JOHN IS SITTING QUIETLY AT HOME IN HIS LIVING ROOM, READING. THE DOORBELL RINGS.

JOHN (TO CAMERA)
Who on earth can this be?

HE OPENS THE FRONT DOOR. CALUM GILHOOLEY BURSTS IN, WEARING HIS BLUE ANORAK AND ARMED WITH A CARRIER BAG.

JOHN (DISMAYED)
Oh, hi Calum.

CALUM
Hi, John, I was just passing in my new car and I thought "I wonder if John's in?" 'cos like I know you live here 'cos like I've been here before and I thought "Well, it's about 9 o'clock" - you could be out at the pub or at the cinema or at a restaurant or some other  hobby I don't know about that takes place in the evening, and then I thought there's no point sitting out here wondering about it, I might as well see if you're in, so I thought I'd park the car. So I saw this parking space, so I put it in reverse, turned round and I reversed in, into the space and parked it, like. And then I got out

of the car, and locked it 'cos it's a new car, like
I told you, and then I got out and went over to
the garden gate, opened the garden gate and I
went through the garden gate and I walked up
the garden path and then I saw your outside
light wasn't on. So I thought, maybe you're not
in after all, and then I thought maybe you are
in but you just haven't got your outside light
on, so I thought I'd ring the bell to find out.
And then I was gonna ring the bell and I saw
that you've got a knocker on your door. And I
didn't know which to do. So I thought, well, it
doesn't really matter 'cos either way you'll
hear me. So, I rang the bell which you probably
heard **(PAUSE)**. So, anyway John, are you in?

JOHN
Yes. **(HE STARES, MOMENTARILY
STUNNED)** Sorry, Calum, come in, come in.
Have a seat.

CALUM
Is that a new couch? It's different from your
last one. Must be a new one, aye.

JOHN
Yeh, it's a new couch.

CALUM
Doesn't look very comfy.

JOHN
I quite like it, Calum. See?

HE RELAXES ON THE SOFA AND INVITES

**CALUM TO JOIN HIM. CALUM SITS DOWN
UNCOMFORTABLY CLOSE TO JOHN.**

CALUM
Oh yeah, it's brilliant. Dead comfy

JOHN
Isn't it?

CALUM
Aye, so do you wanna see see my new car?

JOHN (ABOUT TO STAND UP)
Yeah, OK, we'll go and have a look at it.

CALUM
No it's OK, John. I've got some photographs
here. We could go through them.

**HE DIGS OUT A FRIGHTENINGLY LARGE
NUMBER OF BUNDLES OF PHOTOGRAPHS
FROM HIS CARRIER BAG**

JOHN
Oh, no, no. We could just go outside and see the
car...

CALUM
No, 'cos it's a way outside and it's a bit cold. I've
got a few photos here and we could just look
through, and maybe we'll start with this lot
John **(UNTIEING ONE BUNDLE AND SHOWING
THEM ONE-BY-ONE)**... Now, that's the whole
car, right? Brilliant, eh? And that's the sunroof
which is brilliant too, especially when the sun's

out, like. And that's the... what's that?... oh,
yeah, that's the ignition. See you put the key
in the ignition and that starts it up. **(MORE
PHOTOS)** There's a few different angles
actually...

**CALUM IS OBLIVIOUS AS JOHN CONFIDES
TO THE CAMERA.**

JOHN
Perhaps I should explain at this stage. This ...
this ... eh, thing is Calum Gilhooley. I played
"Subbuteo" with Calum when I was seven and
I can't seem to get rid of him. I just cannot
actually seem to shake him off. Maybe you
think this isn't so bad -but if you could just
imagine that three hours have passed. Three
hours.

**HE RETURNS TO THE SOFA AND SLUMPS
SEMI-CONSCIOUSLY NEXT TO CALUM WHO
IS STILL GIVING AN INCH BY INCH
PHOTOGRAPHIC LECTURE ON HIS CAR ...**

CALUM
... and then that's the bumper from
underneath, looking up at the bumper, looking
at it, aye. I tell you it's brilliant.

JOHN LEAPS BACK UP TO THE CAMERA

JOHN
You see, "brilliant" is the key word for Calum.
Everything in Calum's life is "brilliant". This is
the only man in the world who had brilliant

verrucas. And certainly the only man who has photographs of them. **(RETURNING TO THE SOFA)** That's not his only trick. This man's a professional. He has other ploys.

CALUM
I saw that Cecil Heseltine on the TV the other day.

JOHN (CONTINUING TO APPEAL TO CAMERA AS CALUM TALKS ON)
Who is this? Who is Cecil Heseltine? Is this Cecil Parkinson? Michael Heseltine? Michael Parkinson? Who is he talking about?

CALUM
'Cos we were watching that "One Flew Over The Cuckoo's Nest".

JOHN
"One Flew Over The Cuckoo's Nest"? How did we get on to that?

CALUM
And it was brilliant.

JOHN
Naturally.

CALUM
It had that actor in it, Jack Williamson ...

JOHN
Nicholson.

CALUM
... he was in this prison ...

JOHN
Hospital

CALUM
... and he was friendly with this big, blind Polish guy.

JOHN
Big, dumb Red Indian guy.

CALUM
And they escaped and they ran off on a train ...

JOHN (JUMPING UP, ANGUISHED)
Oh God! No they didn't. I just wanted a quiet night in and suddenly I'm thrust into a remake of "The Creature from The Black Lagoon". And there's nothing you can do to make him realise that perhaps it's time to go.

CALUM (LOOKING AT HIS WATCH)
Oh, is that the time? It's coming on for midnight.

JOHN (TO CALUM)
Yes, it's coming on for midnight.

CALUM
Great, 'cos there's a Davey Bond film on at half twelve.

JOHN
OK Calum. We'll watch the "Davey Bond" movie. **(TO CAMERA)** Because that's what

you say - "We'll watch the Davey Bond movie". When what you really want to say is this - **(TO CALUM)** Calum, are you going to be here much longer?

CALUM
Aye, just for a wee while ... no more than a couple of days, anyway ...

JOHN
OK. Would you like to buy my flat for £10?

CALUM (SUSPICIOUS)
£10? Well, I haven't had a survey done ... but I could take a chance.

JOHN
Do you want to take that chance, Calum?

CALUM
Aye ... OK.

JOHN
Here's the keys!

CALUM HANDS OVER £10 TO A RELIEVED JOHN

CALUM
£10

JOHN
OK. I hope you'll be very happy. I'll just get my stuff.

HE EXITS.

LITTLE GIRL - Queen

Yes, I know what the Queen does. She is the King of all the country and the world and the universe. And she can see everything wot is happening in everywhere febus she has the special glasses wot was given her by ... by ... by Jesus. Yes. And she is the boss of the world. But if she likes she can do anything wot she wants. But you had to listen to her foss if you didn't then she might chop your head off. She might chop it off with a really sharp knife wot she keeps in the drawer and wot gets sharpened by the servant, who wears the shoes. And the Queen is very, very pretty and she wears lipstick and she is ... um ... twenty ... no thirt ... no, fifty, no she isn't any old because the Queen does not ever die or be sick. And the other thing wot the Queen does not never do is she does not go to the toilet. She doesn't. It's true. And the Queen wears the very special fluffy hat with diamonds and rubies and gold and material. And it costs a hundred pounds

... and 25 million pounds. So nobody
must steal it.

But once a robber did steal it. And the
Queen said, "Quickly get the police". No,
wait a minute cos I think that the police
live in the Queen's house in case there is
a war. Or the bomb. Yes, anyway and the
police they do live in the Queen's garden
in little weeny boxes and they wear
really big, huge, enormous big black
furry hats yes they do, and they are not
allowed to ever take them off. If the
Queen blows the whistle then they run
and run and run and they get in the van
wot is a special van wot has the holes
cut out of the top so they can wear the
furry hats in case they get a nasty
bump ...

And then they chase after the robber.
But the Queen stays at home and gives
the lunch to poor black babies. And they
have soup.

And then anyway when they find the
thief and they find him he is hiding in a
monkey's cave and when they find him
they shout "Quickly, get the ... get the ...
get the thing". And the policemen wot
has the biggest furry hat says to the
robber "You're a very very naughty boy
and you will get a punch." And then they
give the hat back to the Queen. And she
says thank you and gives them some
money and a present. It's true. I know
because I do.

THE NICE FAMILY - Points Of View

THE NICE FAMILY KITCHEN, WHERE ALL ARE GATHERED, EXCEPT FATHER. HE ENTERS, HOT UNDER THE COLLAR, CARRYING THE FAMILY TELEVISION SET. HE PLACES IT BY THE SIDE OF THE SINK, WHERE MOTHER IS, AS EVER, WASHING UP.

FATHER
Mother - wash that immediately! To think, showing fire engines on television at 6 o'clock in the evening! Whatever next? Well, family. I think it's high time once and for all that we finished our letter to "Points of View", the interesting television programme.

THE FAMILY APPLAUDS.

FATHER
Now, where on earth did I put it? Ah, here it is. Now, shall I read the letter so far?

ALL
Yes please, father.

FATHER
(COUGHS) Dear "Points of View" ... comma. Well, so far so good, eh? Now

does anyone have any ideas how we
might continue this letter?

**THE CHILDREN ALL THINK AS ONE
FOR A MOMENT, THEN ...**

TWIN 2
Why?

TWIN 1
Oh why?

DAUGHTER
Oh why?

ELDEST
Oh why?

FATHER
Oh why? Splendid! How clever and original.

THERE IS MUCH LAUGHTER AT THE SPLENDOUR OF THEIR JOKE, UNTIL A FATHERLY COUGH CALLS FOR ORDER.

FATHER
'Dear "Points of View". It has come to my wife's attention that during the "Six O'Clock News" Nicholas Witchell, beneath his suit, and underpants, is quite naked. Considering the nature and time of the broadcast, couldn't he at least do the decent thing and wear another suit beneath his underwear? After all, Andrew Harvey seems to manage it.'

ELDEST
Spoken well, father.

FATHER
Thank you, eldest son. Now, any other suggestions?

DAUGHTER
Yes. What about a television programme
based on the popular magazine, "Look and
Learn"? It might, perhaps, be called "Look
and Learn" and last 10 hours.

FATHER
Well, I think that's what they call in the
business 'a rollicking good idea'.
(BACK TO THE LETTER)
'Now, furthermore, the younger members
of my family, collectively known as the
fruit of my loins, would like a new
programme based on "The Observer's Big
Boys' Book of Birds". Now, it might,
perhaps, be called "The Observer's Big
Boys Television Programme of Birds" and
have a theme tune as follows ... **(HE
HUMS THE THEME FROM "VAN DER
VALK")** as the clever Dutchman without
the beard no longer seems to need it.'

**EMULATING THEIR FATHER'S "BRAIN-
STORMING", THE CHILDREN GET
INCREASINGLY CARRIED AWAY ...**

ELDEST
And why not show "The Forsyte Saga"?
After all, it's only 25 years old.

DAUGHTER
Yes, and "The Onedin Line", with its
marvellous theme tune - and it's theme
tune.

ELDEST
Why not combine the two, and have "The
Forsyte Saga" with "The Onedin Line's"
theme tune?

DAUGHTER
Yes, that would keep everyone happy.

TWIN 1
Especially if it had Bob Wilson in it.

TWIN 2
Bob Wilson is just what "The Forsyte
Saga" needs to put some life back into its
feet!

TWIN 1
Can you imagine - the witty asides ...

TWIN 2
His insights into association football ...

FATHER
Now, now, enough, enough. Careful,
family. This letter to "Points Of View" is
in danger of turning into a ... long letter
to "Points Of View", if we're not careful.
Off to your rooms now, and I'll be up
shortly with tonight's general knowledge
quiz.

FOOT AND EAR

**A HOSPITAL WARD. A DOCTOR WALKS UP TO
A MIDDLE-AGED WOMAN WHO HAS BEEN
WAITING FOR HIM.**

DOCTOR
Ah, Mrs Johnson. I'm afraid your husband has
suffered shocking injuries. We've done what we
can, but it has meant rather extensive surgery.

MRS JOHNSON
What have they done?

DOCTOR
Well, Mrs Johnson, we've had to remove quite
a lot of your husband.

MRS JOHNSON
You mean, cut bits off?

DOCTOR
That sort of thing, yes.

MRS JOHNSON
Can I see him?

DOCTOR
Yes, of course ... he's in this bed.

**HE INDICATES WHAT APPEARS TO BE AN
EMPTY BED.**

MRS JOHNSON
What, this one?

DOCTOR
Yes.

MRS JOHNSON
There's no-one there.

DOCTOR
Yes there is - up there, by the pillow.

HE PULLS BACK THE BEDCLOTHES TO REVEAL A FOOT WITH AN EAR SEWN ON IT.

MRS JOHNSON (LOOKING REVOLTED)
OH MY GOD!

DOCTOR
Sssh! He's asleep.

MRS JOHNSON
What?

DOCTOR
That's Mr Johnson's left foot, Mrs Johnson. I'm afraid we could only manage to save that, and his ear.

MRS JOHNSON
His ear?

DOCTOR
Yes. They've sewn it on to the front. Tricky bit of surgery. He can hear every word you say.

MRS JOHNSON (LOWERING HER VOICE)
Is that all that's left of him?

DOCTOR
Mr Johnson... is very lucky to be alive. He's
only survived at all because he's extremely fit.

MRS JOHNSON
He's very keen on body building.

DOCTOR
Good, good. That will come in handy now.
Obviously there may be some psychological
problems. We do find that patients who've had
this sort of surgery tend to get a bit depressed
and withdrawn. He may be reluctant to leave
the house.

MRS JOHNSON
When will he be able to go home?

DOCTOR
You can take him today.

MRS JOHNSON
I haven't got a car.

DOCTOR
That's alright - you can pop him in your
shopping bag.

MRS JOHNSON
Shouldn't he be in a wheelchair?

DOCTOR
Oh, no, no. You don't want to start treating him
like an invalid.

MRS JOHNSON

But, surely, in his condition...?

DOCTOR

Mrs Johnson, when he leaves here he may have a slight limp, but that's all.

(HE LOOKS CLOSELY AT THE FOOT)

Ah yes, I think he's waking up now, so I'll leave you two together.

(HE TAKES HER TO ONE SIDE)

Mrs Johnson, your husband doesn't actually know what we've done to him, and...er... we were wondering if perhaps you wouldn't mind breaking the news, as it were?

MRS JOHNSON

What should I say?

DOCTOR

Break it gently. Perhaps start by saying that we've taken his tonsils out, and then sort of work on from that.

MRS JOHNSON

I'll do my best not to upset him.

DOCTOR

That's the spirit! I've got to go and have a look at a piece of skin in the next ward now, but do call a nurse if you need any help.

MRS JOHNSON

I don't know how to thank you, Doctor ... and neither does Mr Johnson.

DENZIL - Shelves

**DENZIL IS STANDING IN HIS LIVING ROOM.
HE IS SINGING. AT THE SAME TIME WE
CAN HEAR, SOMEWHERE, THE SOUND OF A
CAT HITTING A WALL SEVERAL TIMES.**

DENZIL
Aaaahhhh.........Aaaahhhh........aaaaaaaaahh
hhhh.... Yes, that are lovely. I enjoyed that.

DENZIL'S WIFE, GWYNNEDD ENTERS.

GWYNNEDD
Hello Denzil.

DENZIL
Hello Gwynnedd. What are you doing here?

GWYNNEDD
I live here.

DENZIL
Well, you could always move out. But I
must say, you are looking very
attractive today. Are you ill?

GWYNNEDD
Yes, I'm sick of the sight of you. I've
just knocked the cat out for the night.

DENZIL
Gwynnedd, Gwynnedd, you're spoiling
that animal.

GWYNNEDD
Well, if you'd let me have children, I
wouldn't have to.

DENZIL
I gave you children, Gwynnedd. And
what did you do with them?

GWYNNEDD
I let them go.

DENZIL
Why did you let them go?

GWYNNEDD
It seemed cruel to keep them in the
house.

DENZIL
Gwynnedd, there are an old saying that
you are what you eat. And you have
obviously eaten something very stupid.

GWYNNEDD
Denzil, I have told you before and I won't
tell you again.

DENZIL (PAUSE)
Oh.

GWYNNEDD (A BIT SHY)
Denzil?

DENZIL
Yes, Gwynnedd?

GWYNNEDD
How would you like to put some shelves
up?

DENZIL
How would I like to put some shelves up?
Do birds have beaks?

GWYNNEDD
The beakless ones haven't.

DENZIL
Yes, Gwynnedd, alright. But the beaked
birds have got beaks, haven't they?

GWYNNEDD
Yes.

DENZIL
Yes, that's right. Well, shelves. I think
this calls for a little celebratory cup of
cheesewater.

**DENZIL TRIES TO SWITCH THE KETTLE
ON, BUT POP MUSIC COMES OUT
INSTEAD.**

DENZIL
Oh flipping heck. Why does this kettle
keep picking up Radio 1?

GWYNNEDD
Never mind that, Denzil. Shelves.

**SHE HOLDS UP A COPY OF "THE JOY OF
SHELVES" FOR HIM.**

DENZIL (SEXILY)
Shelves....

**HE REACHES FOR THE TOASTER
SWITCH AND PUTS OUT THE LIGHTS.**

SJFA CUP DRAW

A VERY SPARSELY ATTENDED PRESS CONFERENCE CALLED BY A PANEL OF FIVE MEN IN BAD SUITS. THEY ALL HAVE MOUSTACHES AND LOOK STERNLY OFFICIAL. AT ONE END OF THEIR TABLE IS POSING A FADING GLAMOUR GIRL IN A TARTY TARTAN OUTFIT, NEXT TO A MODEST GREEN BAIZE BOARD LABELLED "QUARTER FINALS DRAW".

ARCHIE

Good afternoon, gentlemen of the press. It's my pleasure to welcome you all here this afternoon to witness, live, as it happens, here and now, in this room... today, the draw for the quarter finals of the Scottish Junior Cup. Now for those of you who don't know, my name is Archie Wilson. I am, in fact, president of the SJFA. And I will be assisted today by my friends here in this onerous and...duty. So, on my left will be Erchie who will be holding the bag containing the coloured balls.

ERCHIE RAISES THE BAG SOLEMNLY.

Thank you very much indeed. Now on Erchie's left there's our very special guest and overseer, Urchie McTash, who is of course, Honorary

Secretary of the SPCRAPFA Association.

URCHIE
My pleasure, Archie.

ARCHIE
And Urchie will be removing the balls from the
bag in his capacity as Honorary Secretary of the
SPCRAPFA Club.

URCHIE
Association.

ARCHIE
**(HE STARES AT URCHIE, NOT SURE WHY HE
HAS SAID "ASSOCIATION".)**
Indeed. Now on Urchie's left is our own Orchie.
Standing in for George. Now George, sadly, can't
be with us this year. George, of course, has sat
in on these proceedings for many years now
and it's a great sadness that he's not here ...
and I think we all hope that he dries out soon.
    And on Orchie's left there's Rchie, who will be
reading out the number of the ball and the
corresponding team name. Now I know this is
very complicated and hope you will bear with us
... oh, I'm sorry, I almost forgot. Of course, we
are assisted this afternoon by the lovely Glenda
who was voted Miss Cumbernauld ... as recently
as 1970. Glenda will be affixing the names to
the "Big Board" as we call it.

**ARCHIE GAZES AT GLENDA FOR A FEW MORE
SECONDS THAN HE PROBABLY SHOULD.**
So, if everyone's ready, we'll have the first ball
please, Erchie.

**ERCHIE GOES TO STAND UP, REALISES THAT
NO-ONE ELSE IS GOING TO, AND SITS.**

ERCHIE
Well, I'll just give the bag a wee shake.

URCHIE
I will now remove the first ball from the bag.

HE PASSES IT ON TO ORCHIE.

URCHIE
I am passing it on to Orchie.

ORCHIE
Thank you Urchie. I am passing the ball on to
Rchie.

RCHIE
Thank you Orchie. I am now passing the ball on to
the lovely Glenda.

**GLENDA TAKES THE BALL AND TRIES TO
STICK IT ON THE BOARD. NOT SUPRISINGLY, IT
DROPS TO THE GROUND AND SHE SCRAMBLES
AROUND ON THE FLOOR AFTER IT.**

ARCHIE
Er ... no...no, Rchie, that's not quite what we had
in mind. If you could read out the number and the
corresponding name ...

RCHIE
(RETRIEVING THE BALL FROM GLENDA)
My mistake, Archie. Sorry. Right, here we go. It's
number 4, er.....Clachnacudden.

GLENDA SLAPS THE NAME ON THE BOARD.

ARCHIE
Interesting, interesting ....
**(HE REALISES THAT NO-ONE IS
INTERESTED)**
Anyway Erchie, let's see who they've got.

ERCHIE IS ASLEEP. ARCHIE NUDGES HIM.

ERCHIE (ABRUPTLY)
I'll just give the bag a wee shake.

URCHIE
I am pulling a numbered ball from the bag ... I
am passing it to Orchie.

ORCHIE
I am receiving the ball and passing it on to
Rchie.

RCHIE
Number 4. Numero... four. Clachnacudden.

**RCHIE LOOKS AT ORCHIE WHO LOOKS AT
ERCHIE WHO LOOKS AT ARCHIE WHO
LOOKS AT THE PRESS.**

ARCHIE
...a fascinating first tie, I think you'll agree.
Anybody's game. Though I must say, of the
two, I fancy Clachnacudden. So, er, let's have a
look at the board ...

**GLENDA IS ON THE FLOOR TRYING
FRANTICALLY TO ALTER A SIGN**

ARCHIE
...Er, no...let's have another ball, Erchie.

ERCHIE
I am holding out the bag.

URCHIE
I am pulling out the next ball... a number ...

HIS HAND IN THE BAG, URCHIE CAN'T FIND ANOTHER BALL.

URCHIE
I am withdrawing my hand from the empty bag.

ERCHIE
I am throwing the bag away.

ORCHIE
I am going for a drink.

RCHIE
I am going for a slash.

ARCHIE
So, there we are then. The draw for the final of the Scottish Junior Cup, and as we can see ...er...

GLENDA HAS QUICKLY RE-ARRANGED THE BOARD. SHE'S CROSSED OUT "QUARTER" AND THE "S" IN "FINALS", AND PUT A NEW SIGN, SAYING "DITTO" NEXT TO THE "CLACHNACUDDEN" SIGN. SHE SEEMS PLEASED WITH HER WORK.

ARCHIE
... between Clachnacudden and Ditto, which promises to be...the end of my term in office.

LITTLE GIRL - Baby Jesus

SHE SINGS

Sweet Baby Jesus. Lying in the manger.
With donkey and the ass and the cattle
and the pony.
And the three Kings comed with
Christmas presents.
For the Baby.
In the swaddley, in the swaddley, in the
swaddley, in the swaddley...
And he got a Cindy dolly, with a twisty
tummy, and another present like my
friend got.

SHE STOPS SINGING

Yes, Christmas is when Mary and Jofus
and the donkey went on holiday to stay
with the King Heron in O little town of
Bethlehem. But when they got there then
it was full up to the brim. And then the
policeman came along and he said "Halt,
who goes there?" and he holded a great
big stick with a poisoned arrow on the
end. What was for killing puppies. And
he said "I am the Roman and you cannot
come in 'fos there isn't any more room."
So they gived him five pounds and they
ran away.

And they ran all the way to Jerusalem
wot is next door to O little town of
Bethlehem and when they got there, they
went into the garage right, and sayed

"three star of the gallons please" and one of the stars of the petrol pump went up in the air and it was the twinkle twinkle little star wot three kings from Africa saw.

Yes, and they saw it and they jumped on a great big stripey giraffe, and they ran all the way to the garage with the presents, and one was Chinese, one was Japanese and one was Pekinese and one was What Are These? **(SHE POINTS TO HER CHEST)**

And anyway, then Mary said "Oh blimey Jofus I think I'm having a baby", and Jofus said "I can't see it" and Mary said "That's fuss it's... a secret. But it is up my bottom." And then Mary did a sneeze and sweet baby Jesus fell on the straw and he said... um, I fink he said "Ding dong merrily on high" 'cos that is what babies do say and then he haved the glass of milk and then he went to sleep 'fus he was very, very tired and babies' eyes do not open for two years. And then Mary singed him a lullaby and he weared the dress. Like the angel's dress, but without the zip. But then the policeman comed along again and he said "You cannot stay in the garage any more", but Jofus said "It's alright 'fus I just bought a pyramid." So they were very happy. And then Jesus grewed up into a big man and got eaten by a lion. And that is Christmas. It's true!

DON & GEORGE - Bargains

GEORGE IS IN THE SITTING ROOM READING A VERY SERIOUS-LOOKING BOOK. DON ENTERS CARRYING A LARGE BOX AND A LARGE CARRIER BAG.

DON
Morning.

GEORGE
Afternoon.

DON
Evening.

GEORGE
Goodnight.

DON
Sleep tight.

GEORGE
Hope the bugs don't bite.

DON
Sweet dreams.

(PAUSE)
GEORGE
Morning.

DON
Morning. What's the book George?

GEORGE
Oh yes, the book. "The Gas Board
Employees Regulations".

DON
Interesting, is it?

GEORGE
Absolutely pa...thetic, Donald. Listen to
this. "Employees are responsible for

laundry and upkeep of their uniforms. It is urged that employees' dress is at all times neat, ironed and, above all, clean."

DON
Who-oah! Sexy stuff, eh?

GEORGE
Sexy, perhaps, Donald, but it's hardly Dickens.

DON
Hardly Dickens? Any relation to Charles Dickens?

GEORGE
Apparently, yes.
(HE READS FROM THE BACK OF THE BOOK)
'Hardly Dickens is the great-nephew of Charles. He was a Gas Board employee for 30 years. This is his first book. He lives in Dorset with a pullover.' So, what's in the box?

DON
I'll show you.

GEORGE
Fair enough.

DON OPENS THE BOX AND PULLS OUT A HIDEOUS SCULPTURE.

DON
There we go. The wee beauty. There you
are.

GEORGE
What is it?

DON
George, it's a bargain.

GEORGE
And what does it do?

DON
What does it do? What do bargains
normally do? It saves us money.

GEORGE
What else does it do?

DON
Isn't that enough?

GEORGE
It just sits there, does it?

DON
It just sits there, saving us money.

GEORGE
How much money does it save us, as it
just sits there doing nothing?

DON

£50, George. And that's not all.

GEORGE

Ah, you have more bargains, do you?

DON

Oh yes.

DON EMPTIES HIS BAG ONTO THE TABLE, TIPPING OUT A HUGE PILE OF PACKETS OF RAZORS.

DON

Free razors! Now this really is an incredible bargain. With every five razors, you get one razor free. Gratis. Free.

GEORGE

Amazing.

DON

Amazing - now that's what I thought. I called over the manager. I said "Do you realise you're giving these razors away?" I said "You're mad man." I shouted at him, I said, "You're mad. You should be certified. This is no way to run a business, but if you're fool enough to do it, then I'm smart enough to take advantage of it."

GEORGE
I see. And what did he say?

DON
He said "Excuse me, sir. I'm afraid I
have to go. The Sanity Express leaves
platform 2 in five minutes."

GEORGE
Sanity? That's in Yorkshire isn't it?

DON
Someplace. Anyway, I took the lot.

GEORGE
Any more surprises for me, Donald?

DON
(HOLDING UP A SET OF KEYS)
...was £1500. Now £1200...

GEORGE
What was?

DON
A car.

GEORGE
Neither of us drives, Donald.

DON
Precisely! No road tax. No insurance. No
petrol. Now that's going to save us up to
£500 a year, add that to the £300
already saved - we're talking almost a

grand. Oh yes, you've got to get up pretty
early in the morning if you want to watch
breakfast TV.

GEORGE
Donald, tell me, just purely as a matter of
interest, when you were in this shop
getting all this stuff, was there anything
you noticed that you did in particular?
Was there any outlay on your part that
might have caught your attention?

DON
Not particularly, no.

GEORGE
Think back man, think!

DON
Well, I caught a bus in to town and back.

GEORGE
No, not the bus. Just before they gave you
these goods, that, granted, have saved us
so much money, what did you do?

DON
Well, I just gave them the money and...
(PENNY DROPS) oh no. I've been duped,
ripped off, taken for a ride. George, I've
been an idiot.

GEORGE
No, no, Donald. You haven't been an idiot.

No, no. You've been a mouse-brained,
senseless, horse's bottom. A category
"A" dribbling, drooling maniac. You have
shamed three millenia of human
progress. You have shown all the
foresight and intelligence of a fence-post.
You would be favouring yourself with an
obscenely over-generous compliment if
you were to merely label yourself an
idiot. Donald, you're a tabloid newspaper.

DON
Thank you very much, George.

GEORGE
Don't mention it. Now how much money
have we saved?

DON
£350.

GEORGE
How much have we spent in order to
make this saving?

DON
(PAUSE) £1450

GEORGE
So, to my reckoning we're £1100 down
on the deal. So, we now have to recoup
£1100. Correct?

DON
Correct. Do you want me to go out and
buy more razors?

GEORGE
No. Donald. That will not be necessary.

GEORGE PICKS UP THE PHONE

DON
What are you doing, George?

GEORGE
I'm going to save us £1100... **(TO
PHONE)** Hello? Globalsun Travel? Yes,
I'm interested in your prices for two
weeks in Marbella.

DON
George!

GEORGE
£900? No, that's not much use. What
about a cruise down the Nile?

DON
No!

GEORGE
£1100? Ideal. Sorry. What was that?
How many people is it for? None! **(HE
PUTS THE PHONE DOWN)** It's easy
when you know how, Donald.

THE NICE FAMILY -
Postie

THE NICE FAMILY KITCHEN. MOTHER, NATURALLY, IS AT THE SINK, WASHING HAMMERS. THE CHILDREN ARE IN SENSIBLE HOME CRAFTS OVERALLS FOR THEIR SENSIBLE HOME CRAFTS-TASKS - CHIEFLY INVOLVING HAMMERING THINGS TO NO OBVIOUS EFFECT.

CAPTION 1: SATURDAY MORNING

CAPTION 2: EARLY

CAPTION 3: ABOUT 5.30 A.M. TO BE PRECISE

AT THE BREAKFAST TABLE, FATHER IS SURVEYING THE MORNING'S POST. HE LOOKS UP. MOTHER IS HOLDING UP A SIGN ANNOUNCING THAT "THE DECAFFEINATED COFFEE FOR YOUR PRE-BREAKFAST DECAAFFEINATED COFFEE BREAK IS ALMOST READY".

FATHER
Family!

THEY STOP HAMMERING.

FATHER

I notice that the de-caffeinated coffee for
our pre-breakfast 5.30 decaffeinated
coffee break is almost ready.

**GASPING FROM THEIR EXERTIONS,
THE CHILDREN WIPE THEIR
FOREHEADS AND SIT DOWN FOR
COFFEE, SERVED, BACKWARDS, BY
MOTHER.**

TWIN 2

That was physically tiring, and yet
physically tiring, nonetheless.

FATHER

Yes, and an excellent start to the day.
And by way of a reward, as they say, I
shall read out the morning's postal
deliveries.

ELDEST

Splendid!

ALL

Yes!

FATHER

Well, we have a postcard from your
mother's sister and brother-in-law in
their collective capacity as your aunt and
uncle who are holidaying at present in
Southern Ireland, as recommended by
Cliff Michelmore, the bald man.

TWIN 1
Apparently it boasts beautiful scenery.

TWIN 2
And time glides slowly by, I've heard.

FATHER
(OPENING A BUFF ENVELOPE)
Yes. But now to more serious matters.
(ALL LOOK SERIOUS IMMEDIATELY)
Excellent ... excellent. An electricity bill.
Oh how excellent! Excellent. This really is
excellent news. According to the Board,
whose method of calculating such matters
is now computerised and, therefore,
failsafe, we have used 375 units this
quarter. Our calculation?

ELDEST
374.

FATHER
We have one unit unaccounted for ... yet
again. This has happened twice in the past
decade! Perhaps it is time we reviewed
our system. Does anyone have any idea as
to the whereabouts of said missing unit?

**THEY ALL SCRATCH THEIR HEADS AND
PONDER THIS MYSTERY.**

TWIN 1
Father, perhaps the Board has made an
error?

THERE IS SHARP INTAKE OF BREATH ALL ROUND, AS THEY STARE IN HORROR AT TWIN 1. MOTHER BREAKS A PLATE.

FATHER
Go to your room!

TWIN 1 LEAVES, DEEPLY UPSET AND ASHAMED.

FATHER
I will not have our nice, happy, smiling and above all, neat, local Electricity Board maligned in such a way.

DAUGHTER (SCARED)
Father. I have a confession to make.

FATHER
Speak up and speak clearly.

DAUGHTER
I was reading late at night ... Burbridge's Encyclopedia of Classic British Insects ... in my excitement ... I fear I forgot to log the extra unit.

FATHER
Well ... in the circumstances, and knowing your fascination with our six-legged friends, who are, after all, God's creatures also ... I shall say no more about it.

DAUGHTER
I apologise. It shan't happen again.

FATHER
The matter is closed. Now, what have we here?

HE OPENS ANOTHER LETTER, STARTS READING IT, THEN SUDDENLY STANDS UP, VERY SHOCKED.

TWIN 2
Is something the matter, father?

FATHER
A summons. I have omitted to pay a parking fine.

ELDEST
Good Heavens!

FATHER
I have shamed the family. I shall, of course, leave immediately.

ELDEST
(STANDING TO PLACE A CONSOLING ARM ROUND HIS PATER)
But surely, father ...

FATHER
Don't touch me! I have sullied the family name. And to think, poor first twin lying upstairs in disgrace!

DAUGHTER (OPTIMISTICALLY)
We can survive ...

FATHER
Hah! I hardly think so - your father
naught but a common criminal. Wife -
pack my bags!

ALL
No!

FATHER
I shall, of course, keep in touch by letter.
But you must not visit me. That much is
clear.

**SOBBING LOUDLY, WITH HER BACK TO
THE CAMERA, MOTHER EXITS
SIDEWAYS.**

FATHER
Look after your mother. I shall never
forget you.

**MOTHER RE-ENTERS SIDEWAYS,
BACKWARDS, CARRYING A SUITCASE.**

FATHER
Mother, are there sufficient underpants?

**MOTHER, STILL SOBBING, NODS THE
BACK OF HER HEAD. ELDEST SON HAS
PICKED UP THE LETTER AND BEGUN
READING IT, WITH MOUNTING JOY.**

ELDEST
Father, ... it ... I ...I can't believe ... it's
wrongly addressed! It's not for you.

FATHER
Can this be true?

DAUGHTER (TAKING THE LETTER)
Yes, it is! Indeed!

FATHER
Oh three hurrahs and God bless Arthur
Negus!

**MOTHER IS BOUNCING ABOUT FOR JOY
IN THE BACKGROUND, AS TWIN 1
ENTERS.**

FATHER
First twin!

ALL
Hurrah! Hurrah!
Hurrah!

TWIN 1
Am I forgiven?

FATHER
God bless you, yes!
Yes! Family! Psalm 23 ....

ALL REJOICING, SING
"The Lord's my shepherd ...etc etc"

"ABSOLUTELY" - Series Two

Transmission: 22nd August - 10th October 1990

Bald Prisoner
Little Girl - Baby
Stoneybridge - Olympics
Adolescent Letter
The Wellses - Black Baby
Bert - Suicide
Bum Book
Denzil - Pregnant
Don & George - Croissants
The Joy Of Age
Old Artist
The Scotsman
Dyslexic Mindreader
Little Girl - Dentist
Calum - In Court
Lawyers Names
The Tour Guide - Alexander Pope
Stoneybridge - Twin Town
Denzil - The Visit

Designer: Margaret Howat
Studio director: Alistair Clark
Film Director and
Series Producer: Alan Nixon

BALD PRISONER

A PRISON GOVERNOR'S OFFICE. A PRISONER ENTERS. THE PRISONER IS BALD.

PRISONER
Hello sir.

GOVERNOR
Hello. How are the
studies coming along?

PRISONER
Fine, fine.

GOVERNOR
Good, good. I hear
that you're the next
John McVicar. The new Jimmy Boyle,
eh? Bit of a writer?

PRISONER
I hope so, sir.

GOVERNOR
Yes.

PRISONER
That's why I gave you my diaries to
have a look at, sir.

GOVERNOR
Ah, yes, indeed. The diaries.

HE OPENS ONE AND READS

"January the first: Bald. January the second: Bald. January the third: Remember to keep going bald. January the fourth: Don't seem to have much hair. January the fifth: Very little in the way of hair. January the sixth: Found some hair ... under my arm, in stark contrast to the top of my head. January the seventh: Got up, had a shave, exercised, went to work in the kitchens. Couldn't help noticing that I've turned into a bit of a slaphead..."

To be honest, they're not the best diaries we've ever had.

PRISONER

But that was before I took up Sociology and English Literature, sir.

GOVERNOR

Oh yes, there is a definite improvement by March.

"The shadows from the barred windows seem to cast their length upon my very soul. The clank of key in lock seems to shut my heart off from all that is good and forgiving. Must man's cruelty and neglect be paraded eternally, or will the ghosts of freedom rise, and lowering their shackles, dance on the grave of inhumanity? Perhaps I should get a wig..."

LITTLE GIRL - Baby

Yes, I do know what happens when your mum haves the baby. She goes into the hosdible and the Doctor says "This way madam" and he puts her in a box, like wot dead people go in. Then he breaks her legs so that the baby can be borned out proply. Then your mum haves a drink to make her sleepy and it is ... um... I think it is beer. And then the Doctor does look in her bottom with the dinoclears and the baby says "I'm ready" and the Doctor does pull out the baby with big tweezers.

Then the Doctor does hold the baby upside down to make it sick, and then he does measure it with the ruler. And when a baby is borned it is only one inch big. With a centimetre on it. And the Doctor does say if it is big enough to go in the world, and if it isn't then he does fold up the baby and put it back up your mum for later. But if it was too big then the Doctor would have to chop your mum's bottom off and do sewing on her tummy in case her meat comes out.

And if it is big enough, then you are allowed to go to the hosdible. And if you are allowed to hold the baby, then you must be very, very careful, because a baby's head is not proply sewed onto the rest of it. And it might drop off and roll on the ground and a dog might eat it.

And your mum would be very cross. And
her face would go blue.

Then it is time for the baby's tea from
your mum's boson. And it has special
cake ... um called baby cake ... and
orange juice. But the baby is not allowed
to see your mum's boson, and that is
why a baby's eyes do not open for two
years.

But when you are holding the baby
you must be careful not to pinch it
because your mum would not like you
any more.

Or punch it. Or spank it. And you must
not bite the baby's nose. Because the
baby needs the nose for when it is
growed up and does the smelling. So you
must love the baby all the time. Yes you
must. It's true.

STONEYBRIDGE - Olympics

OPENS WITH STONEYBRIDGE OLYMPICS BID VIDEO

VOICE-OVER (WITH FEEBLE STONEYBRIDGE SLIDES)

Stoneybridge. Described by Sir Walter Scott as ... Stoneybridge.

Stoneybridge, with its ... stoney bridge.

Stoneybridge. Prospective host for the 1996 Olympic Games.

SLIDE OF BRIDGE
Just look at our facilities. There's our
stoney bridge.

SLIDE OF WASTE GROUND
Our public park with plenty of scope for
development of a track.

SLIDE OF BUILDING SITE
Our swimming pool.

SLIDE OF WASTEGROUND AGAIN
We don't have a velodrome yet but
Maigret does have a bicycle, so you can't
fault us for spirit in ...Stoneybridge

WE SEE A SLIDE OF TABBY (CAT)
Oh...I don't think you're entered in any
competition, Tabby.
    You see everyone wants to get in on
the act in Stoneybridge.

SLIDE OF OLD MAN
If being old and quite interesting was an
Olympic Sport then surely Wully
MacPhee would be there or thereabouts.
    If we could get him out of the pub.

SLIDE OF HOTEL
    Oh...what's this? Of course, it's the
Olympic Village. Or hotel as we call it...
and outside, for the press...

SLIDE OF TELEPHONE BOX
...a first class payphone with its
own...directory. Remember it's 041 22
65601 for Stoneybridge.

SLIDE OF LEANING TOWER OF PISA
All roads lead to Rome, apart from the
B7193 which just skirts Stoneybridge.
   Stoneybridge. Bang slap on the route
of the No. 47 bus. Except for Thursdays
when you'd be advised to change at the
Yetts of Muckart. Or walk.

   Stoneybridge.
   We're Games if you are.

**THE VIDEO ENDS. ON THE TV SCREEN
WE SEE THE CREDITS. STONEYBRIDGE
OLYMPIC BID. ©. SCOTTYFILMS (inc.
HAGGISOUND)MUSIC, THE MACMACS
NARRATED BY FINDLAY STOVEY**

**THERE IS MUCH APPLAUSE FROM THE
COUNCILLORS.**

ALL
Marvellous, etc.

WULLY
Rubbish.

BRUCE
What's the matter Wully?

WULLY

Too short. It was just getting going I thought.

BRUCE

Wully, we're on a tight budget, as you know.

MAIGRET (IN A SMALL POINTED BEARD)

Eh, two points. Secondly, do I have to wear this beard?

ERCH

Maigret, we've been through this before.
    It's traditional. The secretary always has a beard.
    Anyway, you look very handsome. Now, your point please.

MAIGRET

Well, I don't want to be a wet blanket, but don't you think we might be over-reaching ourselves a wee bit with this Olympic bid?

ALL

Tut, tut, tut, Maigret.

BOABY

What would you have us bid for, Maigret?

MAIGRET
What about the Commonwealth Games?
They're crap.

ERCH
Oh no, I think there might be a danger
there. There'd be an influx of ... er, you
know ... other people, shall we say?

BRUCE
I don't quite follow..

WULLY
You know, the sort of people that your
brother-in-law doesn't care for.

BRUCE
Oh I see. Others.

WULLY
Not that it bothers me.

ALL
No, no, no.

BOABY
Anyway, I don't think Alec allows them
in the hotel.

BRUCE
Well look, we've shelled out the twenty
quid for the video. We've got to bid for
something.

EK
What about the Stoneybridge Highland
Games?

ERCH
I think it's jingle time!

ALL
Ooooooh...

SIX YEARS LATER.

**MAIGRET'S BEARD IS NOW
EXTREMELY LENGTHY. WULLY'S SEAT
IS EMPTY.**

MAIGRET
...it's just a wee bit impractical, that's all
I'm saying.

BRUCE
Maigret, Maigret, shut up about the
beard. Boaby here's got the jingles. Well
done, Boaby, by the way, you've really
rushed them through this time.

BOABY
Thanks. OK, is everybody ready? Here
we go.

JINGLE
> It could be Timbuktoo
> Or Paris or even Thailand
> But there's only one place,
> And that's Stoneybridge
> For the Highland
> ...Games

BOABY
Wait a minute! There's one more.

JINGLE
> If you like tossing a caber
> Or eating porridge
> Have the Highland Games
> At Stoneybridge
> And not at Norwich

ALL
Marvellous, etc.

WULLY ENTERS WITH A LETTER.

WULLY (EXCITED)
Here we are! Here's our answer.
"Dear Stoneybridge Town Council.
After careful consideration we are delighted to announce that this year's Stoneybridge Highland Games will be held the week commencing 19th July ... in the Yetts of Muckart".

ADOLESCENT LETTER

A SMALL, DARK ATTIC ROOM, DECORATED WITH POEMS, DRIED FLOWERS, OLD PHOTOGRAPHS, AND LOTS OF SCARVES, ETC. AN ADOLESCENT GIRL SITS AT A TABLE, WRITING IN CANDLELIGHT.

"My darling boy. It must now be over between us. Our love has faded, the jewelled lamp that we once lit with the shapely taper of eternity has turned to its last ember and as it glows in the iridescent firelight, I see your laughing face. But now our love has wandered up the lingering love-lorn lane of impossibility, the strange man in the bowler hat claps his hands and plays a tuneful timbali on his multi-coloured bag-pipes, the birds stop singing their song of sibilant silence and fly south, and with them they take our love. Oh, I am falling, falling, falling down into the mud and filth of selfless sorrow. My God, my God, why has thou forsaken me?" **(TO HERSELF)** That bit's good.

"Oh Baz, I so wanted to be myself with you. Were you yourself with me? Or were you someone else? And if you were someone else, who were you? Were you your brother? Or were you your father?

And where were you when I wondered where you were and couldn't find you?

Perhaps you were the man down the road who has a small dog called Pepe. Are you that man? A little man with a dog? Is that you? I don't know who you are. Does anybody know who they are? I know who I am. I am someone who wants to know who you are. And when you know who you are, if it's different to who you were, let me know. But don't think that I'm sitting beside the telephone, because I'm not. Because there isn't a chair there. And so goodbye. Or is it au revoir, or adieu, or arriverderci or biennvenue? ... and I don't know what it is in German. We haven't done declensions yet. Yours forever, Louise.

P.S. Going out with you was the happiest week of my life."

THE WELLSES -
Black Baby

**PETER AND JENNIFER WELLS ARE A
MIDDLE CLASS COUPLE WITH MIDDLE
CLASS CLOTHES AND MIDDLE CLASS
ACCENTS. JENNIFER IS EXCITEDLY
BRANDISHING AN ENVELOPE AS
PETER ENTERS THEIR MIDDLE CLASS
SITTING ROOM.**

JENNIFER
Oh, Peter, it's arrived. We've got one!

PETER
Got one what?

JENNIFER
Our Kenyan baby. You remember, we
sent off from that advert in the paper ...
"Adopt a ..."

PETER
Oh, yes. Wonderful. Let me see.

**JENNIFER (HANDING HIM SOME OF
THE BUMF)**
There you are.

**THEY START SKIMMING THROUGH
THE ENVELOPE'S CONTENTS.
JENNIFER SEEMS A LITTLE
DISAPPOINTED...**

JENNIFER
Oh...how strange...his name is Jeffrey....

PETER
Oh dear. I'd expected something slightly more ethnicy ...

JENNIFER
I know. What's his surname?

PETER (PEERING AT A DOCUMENT)
Menzies?

JENNIFER
My God, he's not Scottish, is he? Let me see... **(SHE TAKES THE LETTER)** Oh, Peter! That's Menezes.

PETER
Oh, Menezes.

JENNIFER
That's much better. Look, this tells us all about him. "Jeffrey is an average boy. He is very cheerful." **(PAUSE)** He's average?

PETER (GRIMACING AT SOME CHILDISH DRAWINGS)
Well, look at these - "Dog", "Tree", "Lady". Cheerful, but excessively stupid.

JENNIFER
Come on, Peter, he's only ... **(READING)**
Oh. He's ten. I thought we were getting a
baby.

PETER
Let's see the photograph. Oh my God. Well,
there's obviously been a dreadful mistake.

JENNIFER (HOPEFULLY)
Is he a cripple?

PETER
No, no, no ... well, see for yourself.

JENNIFER
Well ... his hair's not as, sort of, curly as I
expected it would be.

PETER
No. He doesn't look ... particularly foreign,
does he?

JENNIFER
He's not really ...

BOTH
Black.

PETER (READING BUMF)
Oh my God. They've given us a Brazilian.

JENNIFER (DISAPPOINTED)
He's not even under-nourished.

PETER

Brazil doesn't need our money. It's all coffee, carnival and football. Marvellous way of life.

JENNIFER

OK. So he's not wearing shoes, but it never did Pele any harm.

PETER

Exactly. Is he any good at sport?

JENNIFER (READING)

It doesn't say ... oh my God.

PETER

What?

JENNIFER

He says we've got to write to him about crop rotation!

PETER

Well, he can stuff that. How much are we paying to educate this dummy? I want a proper one. Get on the phone.

SHE DOES.

JENNIFER

Hello? Is that ActionCrisisAid? Hello, Jennifer Wells here. There seems to have been a bit of a mistake. You've sent us a rather healthy Brazilian adult when

what we were actually in the market
for ... what? **(TO PETER)** She's saying
something about a Columbian?

PETER
No, no. Give it to me. **(HE GRABS THE
PHONE)**
 Hello, Peter Wells here. Now listen - a
South American simply isn't on, OK? We
want an African.

JENNIFER
One with flies in the desert.

PETER
Have you got anyone left from the Band
Aid video? Oh heavens, we're only trying
to help. All we want is a tiny, hungry
African that we can feed up a bit and
encourage to run in the Olympic Games.
Not a corpulent giant who's going to
witter on about crop rotation...
(ACTIONCRISISAID HAVE HUNG UP)
Well, thank you. If they don't want our
money, we'll see if we can get a better
deal with the NSPCC.

JENNIFER
But what will we do about Jeffrey?

PETER
Oh, just write and tell him we're dead.

BERT - Suicide

**WE ARE IN BERT'S HORRIBLE OLD KITCHEN.
HE IS READING ALOUD A LETTER HE HAS
WRITTEN.**

BERT

"Dear...Buggers. I've
decided to do myself in.
There don't seem to be
anything worth living for.
And even if there was, it
would have bloody well
moved by the time I got
there.

I've had a good life, apart from my legs,
which have been bloody shocking. If there's one
thing I can't stand, I can't stand up.

It's my own fault, I suppose. I had too much
quim when I was a young man, and if there's
one thing that's bad for your legs, it's quim. But
I'm passed it now. I haven't had my end away
in months. There's that daft saying about the
widow's mite. Yes, they might, but in my
experience they never bloody do.

Anyway, it'll be a relief not to have to go to
that bloody day centre any more. I hates that
place. At the front door they got this big sack.
And we all had to put our teeth in it. So that
there was no trouble. You never knew where
your teeth had been.

Yes. It's only the thought of death that keeps
me going. I ain't afraid of dying. What I'm
afraid of is getting caught in the automatic

doors on the bus.

Those bastards snatched an old bloke's pension book the other day and it ain't happening to me. Must go now. My circulation stops around about 5 o'clock.

Yours sincerely, Bert Bastard."

Good, I'll post you.

HE PICKS UP AND LICKS THE ENVELOPE, WHICH STICKS TO HIS MOUSTACHE. FOR A MOMENT HE CAN'T WORK OUT WHERE IT'S GONE. THE LETTER GOES INTO THE ENVELOPE AND THE ENVELOPE IS SEALED. HE PICKS UP, LICKS AND SWALLOWS A STAMP.

Arse! I've swallowed him. I've swallowed my last first class stamp. Oh, it'll come out first thing in the morning. I'll post you then.

HE PUTS THE LETTER ON THE FRIDGE, PROPPED AGAINST THE WALL. THE LETTER FALLS DOWN BEHIND THE FRIDGE.

You bloody bugger! You did that on purpose, you bastard. I'll bloody have you. I'll commit suicide if it bloody well kills me.

Oh. That's quite amusing, that is. Har, har, har. That's quite funny.

WE LEAVE BERT ENJOYING A GOOD LAUGH.

BUM BOOK

**A MAN, WHO IS CLEARLY SUFFERING
SOME PHYSICAL DISCOMFORT,
ENTERS A DOCTOR'S SURGERY**

PATIENT
Hello Doctor.

HE SITS, CAREFULLY.

DOCTOR
Hello. Now how can I help you?

PATIENT
Well, it's a bit embarrassing, Doctor. I've
got a library book up my arse.

DOCTOR
A library book up your arse! Good
heavens! What book is it?

PATIENT
It's the latest
Jeffrey Archer.

DOCTOR
That is
embarrassing.
Hardback or
paperback?

PATIENT
Hardback.

DOCTOR
That's a bit of a problem.

PATIENT
I'll say it is. It's due back tomorrow.

DOCTOR
How did it happen?

PATIENT
How should I know? I only joined the library a week ago.

DOCTOR
Oh, don't worry. There's a lot of it about. I had a chap the other week with a magazine up his knob. I wish people would pay more attention to what they're reading. Anyway, I'm going to give you this pamphlet on safe literature and let nature take its course.

PATIENT
Aren't you going to do anything else?

DOCTOR
No need. Just wait six months and it'll come out as a paperback.

PATIENT
Doctor, I don't know how to thank you.

DOCTOR
Really? Well, I'll make an appointment for you to see our speech therapist.

DENZIL - Pregnant

**WE ARE IN DENZIL'S LIVING ROOM,
WHICH IS STREWN WITH THE
WRECKAGE OF HIS DIY PURSUITS.
THERE IS A HOLE IN THE MIDDLE OF
THE FLOOR. SURROUNDED BY A ROAD-
DIGGER'S CANVAS GUARD, DENZIL IS
SEATED, READING A NEWSPAPER.**

DENZIL
I don't know! Wood nine pence a foot.
They must think I'm mad.

**GWYNNEDD ENTERS, BUZZING
LOUDLY AND ZOOMING ROUND THE
ROOM IN THE MANNER OF A
BLUEBOTTLE.**

DENZIL

Flippin 'eck, Gwynnedd! You're not
swarming again, are you?

**HE ROLLS UP HIS NEWSPAPER, CHASES
HER ROUND THE ROOM AND SWATS
HER DOWN.**

GWYNNEDD

Oh, thank you, Denzil.

DENZIL

You want to be very careful, Gwynnedd.
You could have fallen into the loft. **(HE
INDICATES THE HOLE IN THE FLOOR)**

GWYNNEDD

Denzil, I thought a loft was supposed to
go in the roof?

DENZIL

How can I put the loft in the roof? I've
already got the cellar up there.

GWYNNEDD

Oh.

DENZIL

Now what in Swansea are the matter
with you, buzzing about all over the
place?

GWYNNEDD

I have just seen Dr. Willseeyounow.

DENZIL

Have you? Where? What are he doing in
the house?

GWYNNEDD

No, Denzil. I seen him up at the surgery.

DENZIL

Gwynnedd, Gwynnedd. What are you
telling me all this for? There are nothing
unnatural about seeing Dr.
Willseeyounow in his own surgery.

GWYNNEDD

No, Denzil. He saw me at the surgery.

DENZIL

Well, he would do, if that's where you
were. Doctors are trained to notice
people moving about in their own
surgeries.

GWYNNEDD

Denzil, Dr. Willseeyounow says we are
going to hear the pitter-patter of tiny
feet.

DENZIL

Ach Y Fi (tr. "How unpleasant!"),
Gwynnedd! You haven't got rats again,
have you? I thought I'd noticed
something scuttling about in your
clothes.

GWYNNEDD
Denzil, that was me.

DENZIL
Well, stop it! I don't like scuttling.
Scurrying are alright. But I can't stand
scuttling.

GWYNNEDD
Denzil, I'm going to have a baby.

DENZIL (NOT PLEASED)
Eeaugh!

GWYNNEDD
Yes, Denzil - eeaugh. I am seventeen
years pregnant.

DENZIL
Seventeen years pregnant! Gwynnedd, if
you have been pregnant for 17 years,
you must have noticed something
unusual, like morning sickness?

GWYNNEDD
I did. But I put that down to waking up
in the same bed as you.

DENZIL
Alright, Gwynnedd, alright. Well. If you
are going to be a mother, then I must be
a ...

GWYNNEDD
Git.

DENZIL
No, Gwynnedd. A father.

GWYNNEDD
Oh no, Denzil. Don't worry. You are not
the father. Nobody are the father.
Nobody have touched me. It are a
miracle.

DENZIL
No, Gwynnedd. It are not a miracle.
What would have been a miracle would
be if somebody had touched you.
(GWYNNEDD LOOKS PAINED)
Anyway, Gwynnedd, when are this baby
due?

GWYNNEDD
Five o'clock.

DENZIL
Five o'clock! Gwynnedd, if you are
expecting a baby at five o'clock, you
certainly shouldn't be standing there
talking to me.

GWYNNEDD
No.

DENZIL
No. Go and make my tea. Quick.

DON & GEORGE - Croissants

A DISGRUNTLED GEORGE ALONE AT HOME READING NEWSPAPER. RIFLING THROUGH, NEARING BACK OF PAPER.

GEORGE
Nothing! Not a mention **(TURNING A PAGE)**. Photo of the Chancellor. Not a sniff. Oh, photo of a man who's evidently adept at kicking a football....I mean why can't they say "The goal was scored by so-and-so but here's a photograph of the lesser known George McDiarmid who you haven't seen before" or a crossword clue even...Dashing Intelligent Scotsman -

ENTER DONALD WITH PLASTIC SHOPPING BAG.
-with idiotic friend, 6, 9.

DON
Morning.

GEORGE
Oh! Morning, is it? In he comes, large as life. "Morning", he says, quite the thing.

DON
Yes, morning.

GEORGE
Oh it's "Yes Morning" now, all of a flash.
Not content with "Morning".

DON
What's up George?

GEORGE
"What's up George?" he says. What's up?
I'll tell you what's up. None of your
bloody business, that's what's up. Where
have you been?

DON (HOLDS UP SHOPPING BAG)
Where do you think?

GEORGE
Inside the bag?

DON
At the shops.

GEORGE
Well, hardly surprising Donald, seeing as
you went out to buy four croissants.

DON
Are you in a bad mood?

GEORGE
No! I'm not in a bad mood. Hungry
maybe.

DON
Well we were lucky to get them. Last
shop I tried.

GEORGE (NOT SURPRISED)
Last shop?

DON
Last shop.

GEORGE
That wouldn't have been the baker's by
any chance?

DON
Did you follow me?

GEORGE
No, just a lucky guess.

DON
Well you're right... first shop I went to...

GEORGE
No, please. Let me see if I can guess the
Donald McDiarmid Croissant Route. Right,
you go out of here, you turn right, you go
down the road, first shop you come to is the
newsagent's...

DON
Precisely. No luck.

GEORGE
Number 2, Halfords.

DON
Didn't even answer me.

GEORGE
I don't suppose you'd have gone past the
betting shop?

DON
No. Ladbrokes was open. At least they
tried. They searched lists for any mention
of four croissants .... nothing.

GEORGE
Number 4, The Bradford and Bingley.

DON
Now she had the cheek to suggest I went
next door ....I explained to her that

naturally I had already been to
Ladbrokes...and stormed out...went the
other way...rather pointedly....

GEORGE
Into the bakery?

DON
Into the bakery. Not expecting anything.
Virtually given up. But they came up
trumps.

GEORGE (SARCASTIC)
The bakery had some croissants!

DON
Yes. No fuss. No lip. I think, in future,
I'll just do all my shopping there.

GEORGE (LOOKING AT THE BAG)
Well?

DON
Fine.

GEORGE
Let's have them.

DON
Oh right... sorry, yes... here we go ...

**EMPTIES BAG ONTO TABLE - FOUR
BICYCLE PUMPS AND A PASS BOOK.**

GEORGE
Looks uncannily like four bicycle pumps
to me.

DON
Don't forget the pass book.

GEORGE
**(AS HE FLICKS THROUGH THE PASS
BOOK)**
OK Donald. What happened?

DON
Well, I went back to the Bradford and
Bingley to apologise for my
rudeness...rather hit it off with the
assistant second time round....opened a
deposit account.

GEORGE
Oh really. So what sort of interest rate
do you get on four croissants?

DON
9.3 per cent.

GEORGE
Well, that's not bad. In six months' time,
you'll have a Chelsea Bun you didn't
have before.

DON
Thought you'd be impressed.

GEORGE
Yes indeed. Very impressed. As for the bicycle pumps. Where do they come in?

DON
Well, you see, I knew you wanted four of something, and I had been a bit rude in Halfords as well, and I thought it would be stupid to leave things on a sour note.

GEORGE
Oh yes... that would be stupid.

DON
Obviously.

GEORGE
And what about buying four bicycle pumps...for breakfast. D'you think the word stupid would apply there?

DON
Not sure on that one, George.

GEORGE
Think about it, four bicycle pumps... heated up....lightly smeared with butter.... the word 'stupid' doesn't float by in any way?

DON (PAUSES)
What does 'stupid" mean again?

GEORGE (STANDS UP)
It means buying four bicycle pumps...

when we already have about 3 million.

**OPENS WARDROBE. ABOUT 3 MILLION
BICYCLE PUMPS FALL OUT.**

DON
We were lucky, they were the last four in
stock.

GEORGE
Of course they were, because the rest of
the stock's here, you bloody idiot.

DON
I thought you were in a bad mood.

GEORGE
I'm not in ... of course I'm in a bad mood.
I haven't had a breakfast for four weeks.

DON
Well me neither. But at least I go out and
try to get some...at least I do that.

GEORGE
Don, you know very well I can't do
anything until I've read the morning paper.

DON
Oh that's it, isn't it...you didn't get a
mention, did you?

GEORGE
No.

DON
Are you sure...have you checked
everywhere?

GEORGE
Everywhere. Even the Deaths column, but
apparently it appears, tragically, I am still
alive. As are you. Do you realise how long
I've been reading that bloody rag?

DON
Ever since I stopped going out to buy it?

GEORGE
Precisely. And I've never had so much as
a mention.

DONALD
Look George, I really think you have to
make things happen.

GEORGE
They say everything comes to he who
waits....unless your name's George bloody
McDiarmid that is ... in which case
...nothing comes.

DON
You got your bicycle pumps.

GEORGE
Shut your face!

THE JOY OF AGE

AN ELEGANT RESTAURANT. FOUR ELDERLY PERSONS - JACK, MORWENNA, JOHN AND PETE - ARE BEING INTERVIEWED BY A YOUNG MAN - MORAY.

JACK

No, no, NO, I'm not having any of this "Here lies, Dearly beloved" rubbish... what I want is a plain headstone with "Dead, dead, dead as you like, thank you very much, goodnight."

MORWENNA

I've already ordered mine. It's a simple engraving.

"Would someone please sue that bastard Dr. Montague-Smith, 45 Harley Street, W1."

Put that in your periodical young man.

YOUNG MAN
Well, you see I'd like to put that in the magazine, but really we want to concentrate on the positive aspects of old age.

PETE
Positive?

YOUNG MAN
Aye, your experiences - you must have loads of brilliant stories to tell ...

PETE
The only story I can tell your readers is what it's like to stand in the middle of Oxford Street screaming "Does anybody know where I live"?

JOHN
I'll tell you something, young man. I'm 75 years of age.

YOUNG MAN
Exactly, that's seventy-five years of living history...

JOHN
Well, that's as maybe, but don't ask me. I can't even remember what I had for my lunch.

JACK
It's turbot old boy.

JOHN
Well there you are, turbot, could be a
fish for all I know.

YOUNG MAN
But in the last 20 years the standard of
living for elderly people has improved
enormously. Look at the advances in
medical science ...

MORWENNA
Well, granted, yes, I've got a pacemaker,
that's fine, keeps me going. Of course
what they don't tell you is that you're
going to spend half your life stuck to the
fridge door along with the magnetic
ladybirds.

JACK
Yes, have a colostomy they said. 'Course
they don't tell you you've got to change
the damn bags yourself.

YOUNG MAN
Surely that's simple enough?

JACK
Simple enough if you remember to take
the spare. Many's the time I've been
wondering round with a crisp packet
stapled to my cummerbund. Once spent
two weeks lugging a bin liner round the
Tuscan Hills.

JOHN

It's the indignity of age I can't stand. I
mean, look at me. I've got two degrees,
I've been on the boards of seven major
corporations, been married four times,
and I get up in the morning, eat my
socks and answer to the name of Susan.
What have you got to worry about ...
only who you had sex with last night.

MORWENNA

Do you know, there's a 50% chance that
by tomorrow I won't be able to spell sex.

JOHN

Let alone spell it ...

YOUNG MAN

Well from my experience, that's surely
an advantage.

JACK

Now listen young man, listen here, put
this in your article. Old age is sad,
lonely, depressing, messy and tedious,
but, and it's a big but, you can do this ...

THE FOUR PICK UP THEIR PLATES AND DUMP THEIR MEALS OVER THE YOUNG MAN'S HEAD

...and put it down to eccentricity.

Cigar anyone?

OLD ARTIST

A FILTHY, SEEDY, BESPATTERED ARTIST'S STUDIO. AT A DILAPIDATED EASEL IS AN OLD ARTIST. IN HER 70S, EQUALLY BESPATTERED AND FILTHY. A YOUNG MALE MODEL SITS NAKED, WITH HIS BACK TO CAMERA, A STRONG YOUNG BACK. THE ARTIST TAKES A DRAG OF CIGARETTE AND COUGHS FURIOUSLY THEN SHE SPITS ONTO HER PALETTE AND RUBS IT IN WITH THE BRUSH. SHE STARTS PAINTING, WILDLY.

You're a very nice young man, aren't you? Very nicely proportioned. Very nice and muscly. Got plenty of manhood about you. Are you homosexual? Don't be shy. Just move your leg a bit. Oh yes, I could give that a good gobble. I used to be renowned in my day. Picasso once said of me, "She paints like a princess and gobbles like a gander". Whatever that means. He was completely barking at the end. I had him, of course. We all did in those days; we were bohemian. Do I shock you?

I used to be a great beauty, you know, oh yes. They all said so. Everyone wanted to paint me. Braque, Cezanne, Leonardo Da Vinci - I had them all. Men, women, animals. Drew the line at Royalty. Clergymen were best -

everything to lose, you see. I never said no
to a cassock. Oh yes, I was very lovely. Do
you find me attractive? Would you like to
kiss me? You want to, but you shan't.
We've got work to do. Oh yes, I am a very
attractive woman. Don't worry if you feel
yourself beginning to get aroused. Oooh,
I'm lovely. Do I attract you?

I'm a legend, you know I never wash, I
eat cat food and I piss in the sink. How old
do you think I am? See, I've managed to
keep my figure. Would you like to see me
naked? Give me some money or I'll take
my clothes off and call the police! I've
always been a friend of scandal. I shot my
husband and I had an affair with Stalin.
He was a very well hung man "heavy with
seed," he used to say. I used to relieve him
every day at noon. It was like a volcano.

Do you think I smell? Some people find
that very attractive. You're a very
attractive young man. After I've finished
this, I'll give you a good going over. Do you
have a girlfriend? Is she pretty? I'll have
her too.

I'm a genius. I used to be in the WRENS.
Oh yes, we've got a fabulous piece of work
here. They're all going to want me when
they see it. They're going to pay thousands
upon millions for it. I'll get to give it to
them all - the dealers, their wives, their
children. Do I shock you?

**SHE THROWS DOWN HER PALETTE AND
BRUSH**

THE SCOTSMAN

TWO SCOTTISH PERSONS ARE MEETING IN A BAR. ONE IS A DAPPER FELLOW IN TARTAN JACKET AND BOW TIE. HE IS SIPPING CAMPARI. THE SCOTSMAN IS UNKEMPT WITH STRAGGLY HAIR AND A DROOPY MOUSTACHE. HE IS DRINKING A LARGE WHISKY AND A PINT. HE WEARS A BERET.

SCOTSMAN
Aye, see what you're sitting on there pal:
you know what you'd be sitting on if it
wasn't for the Scots. Your arse. That's
what you'd be sitting on.

MAN
Is that right?

SCOTSMAN
Aye, it was Dougal ... Dougal... **(MAKING
IT UP)** of up by..., in the 16th century,
the first guy ever to sit down on
something other than just his arse. He
invented the chair. Did.

MAN
I'm sure he did.

SCOTSMAN
Aye, and then the English came up and
stole that idea, went back south and said

"What about this then, this chair thing
we've just invented?" Well, they didn't. It
was us. We invented it. Just like every
other bloody thing.

MAN
Well, that's very interesting.

**THE MAN TAKES A SIP OF HIS
CAMPARI, AND LICKS HIS LIPS.**

SCOTSMAN
Aye, see what you've just done there,
that's down to us too. Aye, that was
Malcolm... Malcolm... in the 17th
century. First guy ever to...

HE LICKS HIS LIPS TOO
...to do that, yeah. Famous nation of lip-
lickers, us. The rest of the world would
be going round with big dribbly lips, if it
wasn't for us. Aye, you didn't know that,
did you?

MAN
I didn't, no.

SCOTSMAN
Aye. You should take an interest in your
nation's achievements, pal. Aye, hats.
That's another thing. We were the first
people ever to drop a bunnet right there
(POINTS TO HIS HEAD)...Frasers of
Glenerp, the Hat Clan as they should be

known, if it wasn't for the bastard
English. **(DISGUSTED)** The English! We
even invented them. We did! We took all
the people in our country who were
poofs or perverts or deviants or bastards
or girls and put them down in the south,
and we said "Right, you can be the
English. You just stay there and we'll
come down and kick your arse every
now and again."

MAN
Well, that's very interesting...

SCOTSMAN
I'll tell you something else interesting.
Ever been abroad, noticed what it's like?

MAN
I haven't really thought.

SCOTSMAN
Looks just like Scotland! Aye, right? You
go to Canada - Scotland. New Zealand?
You could be in Paisley. The Galapagos
Islands? Look just like the Isle of Eigg -
without the Bennett's Bar. Aye. The
bastards even stole our idea for the
countryside.

MAN
Yes.

SCOTSMAN

And another thing. There's five million people in Scotland. Do you know how many people there are in the world of Scots descent?

MAN

I don't.

SCOTSMAN

Forty billion. Aye, that's right. Forty billion.

MAN

There aren't forty billion people in the world.

SCOTSMAN

Says who? Aye, says the English. 'Cos they don't want anyone to know that we're everywhere, doing everything. Everything in the world is down to Scots, right? Dehydrated space food - a Scotsman. Bootlaces. Drainpipes. Dymo-tape. Us. Those fiddly twiddly little toggle buttons. The Olympic Games. Curtains, Shopping. The Country Code. The Extra Puffy pillow. It was Scotsmen!

MAN

That's very interesting, Mr MacGlashan, but we really must get down to business.

HE TAKES OUT A SCRIPTS FILE.

SCOTSMAN
Aye, OK.

MAN
Now, I'm afraid that the board has
decided that the West End just isn't
ready for "Whoops My Kilt!"

SCOTSMAN
What about "Hoots Mon! Here Comes
Bonny Prince Chuggy"?

MAN
'Fraid not.

SCOTSMAN
Ah, bugger.

DYSLEXIC MINDREADER

A MINDREADER, "THE GREAT THINKO", IS PERFORMING HIS ACT ON THE STREET, TRYING TO ATTRACT A CROWD.

THINKO

Gather round! Gather round! Thank you, ladies and gentlemen. I am The Great Thinko, and I have an amazing ability. The ability to read minds. Unfortunately, I have a problem. I am dyslexic. However, I have overcome this problem to become The Great Thinko. May I have a volunteer please? You.

HE GRABS A BLOKE WHO DOESN'T LOOK AMUSED TO HAVE BEEN SINGLED OUT. THINKO PUTS ONE HAND ON THE MAN'S HEAD AND ... READS, MENTALLY.

THINKO

I feel something coming up! Something is coming up...

Fuff ock, yon bastand.

I think there is a message there for all of us.

LITTLE GIRL - Dentist

Yes, I do know what happens when you go to
the Densists. You must go with your mum
and sit in a brown room wot smells like a
cough sweet wot has fallen down the toilet.
And this is where you do the waiting for the
lady wot looks like a nurse but is not really
a nurse to come and get you. And when you
are in this
changing room
you must be
very quiet. And
your mum does
read a
magazine with
pages
dropping out,
and cooking
on it, and
you are
allowed to
look at the
pictures on the wall, and you can
see a picture of a big toothbrush wot is
maked into a boy wot can talk, and you
must not scribble on it.

Then the lady does come and get you and
says it is time to go in the special tiny room.
And there's a big chair in it wot is looking
like a bed, but has no blankets, and it's got
electric in it and it will kill you if you cry.
And you can see the Densist's table and it
haves got scissors and knifes and forks on

it, and they are for chopping off your
tongue with. And they do get sharpened by
a little Dwarf wot lives in a cage. Anyway
then the Densist does smile and do say "Do
not be very frightened, please, thank you,
febus I'm only going to have a look for
heaven's sake". And then you must open
your mouth really wide enough for a
puppy to go in.

Then he does bend over and you can see
his hairy nose, and skin does fall out of his
hair onto your jumper, and his mouth does
smell all pooey, and he must have very
brown teeth, with shiny bits, but it is
alright febus he is the Densist. And then
he does tell you to open your mouth even
bigger. That is febus he wants to get in
your throat and have an adventure. But
he is too big. And then he does say to the
pretend nurse "Look madam this tooth is
made out of milk so you must be very
careful. And this one is made out of gums.
And this one has got a great big hole in it"
and then he is very angry and he does
punch you on the tongue with the pliers.
And then the pretend nurse she does make
you try to drink poison. And it is red, and
you must never ever swallow it, febus if
you do, your throat will shrivel up into a
snake wot will crawl into your tummy and
turn into a tape-measure. And it will only
die if you let it eat Mars bars. And that is
what happens when you go the Densists. It
is. It's true.

CALUM - In Court

**CALUM STANDING IN THE DOCK. THE
PROSECUTOR IS APPROACHING HIM.
JACK IS CHIEF WITNESS.**

PROS.
Is your name Calum Gilhooley?

CALUM
Aye.

PROS.
Do you reside at 34 Polwarth Gardens?

CALUM
Aye. How do you know that?

PROS.
It's my job to know that.

CALUM
Is that what you do for a living? Just
know my address? Who pays you?

PROS.
I understand that you are aged 28 and
are currently employed as a barman.

CALUM
Have you been following me?

PROS.
I take it you understand the charges?

CALUM
No.

PROS.
You understand how you came to be in
the court?

CALUM
Aye, I got the 24 bus...hung around
outside...then came in through that door
over there.

PROS.
Mr Gilhooley, you are charged that

continuously, from the moment you first
met my client, you have harassed him
with your conversation, with phone calls
and with anecdotes about your motor bike.
Furthermore, on numerous occasions, you
have rendered my client senseless with
boredom, to the point where he now
screams whenever his phone rings, will
only go out dressed in a balaclava and
sun-glasses, and on one occasion sold you
his flat for £10 rather than watch, and I
quote, a "Davey Bond" movie with you. Mr
Gilhooley, how do you plead?

CALUM STARES STRAIGHT AHEAD.

Mr Gilhooley. Look... **(PROSECUTOR
HOLDS OUT HIS HAND IN
EXASPERATION.)**

CALUM (INSPECTING HAND)
What is it?

PROS. (STILL WITH HAND OUT)
No, listen ...**(CALUM IS PUTTING HIS
EAR TO THE OUTSTRETCHED HAND)**...
no, to me ... here.

CALUM (LOOKING BACK UP)
Sorry. I was just wondering why you wear
that wig 'cos it's no because you're bald
'cos I can see you've got plenty of hair,
and then I thought, well, maybe it was a
present or a joke or maybe you wear it to

make you look taller ... or to make you look like you've got a wig on, which it does by the way, and then I thought it's none of my business, I mean, you don't ask me why I wear an anorak, which I appreciate but I don't mind telling you seeing as you're asking, the reason being that I like it, I prefer it and it's got lot of pockets. **(HE OPENS THEM TO SHOW THEM OFF)**

JACK (LEANS FORWARD TO PROSCEUTOR)
See what I mean?

CALUM
Oh, hi John ... thanks for coming to support me, I don't know what's going on here, this guy seems to have been following me. I think it's 'cos he likes my anorak. To be honest, I think he's a bit of a weirdo, what with the wig and all that, still I think I've got him on the run.

PROS.
Mr Gilhooley, it's your friend here that's brought the charges - it's him you've bored to death.

CALUM
(LAUGHS) Oh John's always doing daft things ... he's a brilliant practical joker...I'll phone him up for ages, and he doesn't answer, then I go round to his

house, he still doesn't answer, then I look in the window, and he's hiding behind the sofa...he's always doing daft things.

PROS.
Mr Gilhooley, do you plead guilty or not guilty?

CALUM
Don't know. What do you do?

PROS.
It would be a lot easier for all of us if you plead guilty...then we could all go home.

CALUM
Oh, that's OK. I don't have to be home for ages. I'll plead the other one.

PROS.
Not guilty?

CALUM
Oh thanks. That was quick. What made you change your mind?

PROS.
I haven't changed my mind. I was asking you what your plea was.

CALUM
Again! Christ, we're going round in circles. Is this your first time?

PROS.
No further questions, Mr Gilhooley.

CALUM
OK. I was only asking if it was your first
time. But if you don't want me to ask any
more questions, I won't.

PROS.
I have no further questions for you.

CALUM
What are we going to do now then?

PROS.
Mr Docherty, would you please take the stand.

JACK GETS INTO WITNESS BOX.

CALUM
It's good fun this, eh, John? It reminds me
of Perry Manson, you know, A Man Called
Fireside, The Lazy Detective, not as good as
the fat one, Columbus, and my favourite,
Kodak.

PROS.
Now Mr Docherty...

CALUM
John, eh, these boxes are great. 'Cos
they're high up, and you can see down...
(HE LOOKS AT THE FLOOR) you've got to be
careful though that you don't go down
yourself ...

**HE DUCKS DOWN INTO THE BOX -
DISAPPEARING**

'cos then you won't see anything ... I mean I
can't see a thing...well, I can see the wood
inside... **(HE STANDS UP)**

PROS.
Please be quiet!

CALUM (WHISPERS)
What is it? I can't hear anything.

PROS.
Mr Docherty, is this Mr Calum Gilhooley?

CALUM
Oh, I like the way he gets the easy ones!

JACK
Yes it is.

PROS.
How long have you known him?

JACK
Since the beginning of time.

PROS.
And you wish this now to stop?

JACK
More than anything.

PROS.
Now I understand that you have a tape
of Mr Gilhooley speaking, which you
would like to play to the court.

JACK
Indeed.

**JACKS HANDS A CASSETTE TO THE
PROSECUTOR WHO POPS IT IN A
MACHINE. WE HEAR CALUM.**

CALUM'S VOICE
Anyway, John, this new stapler I was
telling you about is brilliant 'cos not only
does it staple things but ... it also ... well
... actually, it _does_ only staple things, but
it staples them really well ... and it's
black and you put the staples inside and
they're dead cheap and last for ages 'cos
I hardly ever use a stapler unless I do,
or maybe lend it to a mate or maybe
take it out in the garden for a walk...

**THE PROSECUTOR SWITCHES OFF THE
TAPE.**

CALUM
Hey, that was interesting I was listening
to that.

PROS. (PICKING UP HIS PAPERS)
So was I...
TO JACK

...you're on your own.

THE PROSECUTOR EXITS.

JACK
Oh God, no!

CALUM
Don't worry John, I'll help you.

JACK
Oh God.

CALUM (LEAVING THE STAND HE APPROACHES THE BENCH)
Now, I don't know, your Honour, what the charges are you've brought against my trumped up friend here ... but I tell you they won't stick 'cos he's brilliant ... and, er ... he's my mate ... and he's brilliant.

JUDGE
Mr Docherty, have you got anything that you'd like to say?

JACK
Yes. Would you please send me to prison.

JUDGE
Good idea. 15 years.

HE LOOKS AT CALUM.

I'll come with you.

LAWYERS NAMES

**A SQUASH CLUB CHANGING ROOM.
TWO CHAPS ENTER AFTER A GAME.
THEY ARE GRADUALLY JOINED BY
OTHER CHAPS.**

RUSSELL
Well played, Derek, well played ... you're
looking good, very good.

DEREK
Thanks, Russell.

RUSSELL
Old boy Johnson's obviously not pushing
you too hard, then?

DEREK
Old boy Johnson? Keep up with the
times, Russell. I'm not with old boy
Johnson any more. Moved on. I'm with
Dickerson, Falconer & Gardiner now.

RUSSELL
Dickerson, Falconer & Gardiner? Jolly
good, jolly good. Hear that James? Derek
here's gone to Dickerson, Falconer &
Gardiner.

JAMES
Really? Is that Gardiner who was with
Adams, Boyd, Little, Smart, Simpkins &
Hopkins?

RUSSELL
No, no, no. That's Willy Gardiner ...
who's gone to Dobson, Hobson, Robson,
Jobson & Smith. No, the Gardiner we're
talking about is Willy Gardiner who's
gone to Brodie, Wilks, Brotchie,
Crawford, Littleton, Dundas, Patrick,
Tardelli and Hobbs.

BOBBY
But I thought Brotchie from Brodie,
Wilks, Brotchie, Crawford, Littleton,
Dundas, Patrick, Tardelli & Hobbs had
gone to Chisholm, Chipchase, Fetterman,
Coker, Arkwright, Stevens, Witherspoon,
Higgs, Biggs & Keltingbrook.

JAMES
He has.

BOBBY
He has? Brotchie from Brodie, Wilks,
Brotchie, Crawford, Littleton, Dundas,
Patrick, Tardelli & Hobbs has gone to
Chisholm, Chipchase, Fetterman, Coker,
Arkwright, Stevens, Witherspoon, Higgs,
Biggs & Keltingbrook?

JAMES
Yes. Young boy Brotchie has.

BOBBY
Young boy Brotchie...?

DEREK
...from Brodie, Wilks, Brotchie,
Crawford, Littleton, Dundas, Patrick,
Tardelli & Hobbs...

RUSSELL
...has joined Chisholm, Chipchase,
Fetterman, Coker, Arkwright, Stevens,
Witherspoon, Higgs, Biggs &
Keltingbrook.

ALEX
Yes.

BOBBY
What about old boy Brotchie, then?

ALEX
Ever come across a mob
called...ehem...Davies...

DEREK
Brown...

RUSSELL
Black...

JAMES
Hatchett...

ALEX
Cratchett...

DEREK
McNiven...

RUSSELL
McStiven...

JAMES
McDriven...

ALEX
Leadbetter...

DEREK
Merril...

RUSSELL
Gass...

JAMES
Bowbrick...

ALEX
Bowbridge...

DEREK
Bowcock...

RUSSELL
Bowcott...

JAMES
Glassett...

ALEX
Waddle...

DEREK
Hoddle...

RUSSELL
Twaddle...

JAMES
Doddle...

ALEX
Dying...

RUSSELL
Dead &...

BOBBY
... Jones, yes. He's joined them, has he?

ALEX
No, no. He's had an offer.

BOBBY
Old Boy Brotchie...?

DEREK
From Brodie, Wilks, Brotchie, Crawford,
Littleton, Dundas, Patrick, Tardelli &
Hobbs...

JAMES
Whose son, young boy Brotchie is with
Chisholm, Chipchase, Fetterman, Coker,
Arkwright, Stevens, Witherspoon, Higgs,
Biggs & Keltingbrook...

RUSSELL
Whose brother-in-law, Willy Gardiner, has
gone to Hobson, Robson, Dobson, Jobson
& Smith...

BOBBY
...has had an offer from Davies, Brown,
Black, Hatchett, Cratchett...

BOBBY/JAMES
...McNiven, McStiven, McDriver,
Leadbetter, Merril, Gass...

BOBBY/JAMES/RUSSELL
Bowbrick, Bowbridge, Bowcock, Bowcott,
Glassett...

BOBBY/JAMES/RUSSELL/DEREK
Waddle, Hoddle, Twaddle, Doddle, Dying,
Dead ... & Jones?

ALEX
Yes.

BOBBY
Is he going to take it?

ALEX
Well, he's not sure. You see, he's had
offers from seven other companies
**(THEY ALL TURN TO FACE THE
CAMERA, SMILING)**
seven other companies larger than the
last one.
(SMILING NOT WITHOUT MENACE)

DEREK
Seven other companies, eh?

RUSSELL
Larger ones, you say?

JAMES
You mean, with longer names?

ALEX
Yup!

DEREK
Well, you'd better tell us what these
companies are called.

ALEX
Right...

**BOBBY (STEPPING FORWARD, BEFORE
ALEX STARTS, UP TO THE CAMERA)**
£10. We start the bidding at £10. <u>Not</u> to
hear seven other company names... £10.
Do I hear £10?...

THE TOUR GUIDE
Alexander Pope

A SMALL, ANCIENT-LOOKING ROOM IN
AN 18TH-CENTURY TOWN HOUSE. IT IS
RICKETY AND SPARSELY FURNISHED
WITH A BED, A DESK AND A CHAIR,
ALL CIRCA 18TH CENTURY OR OLDER.
THERE IS ALSO A MULTI-PANED
WINDOW. THE TOUR GUIDE IS A VERY
DOTTY-LOOKING LITTLE
WOMAN IS
SHOWING
ROUND A
GROUP OF
TOURISTS.
THE ROOM IS
VERY
CRAMPED. THE
WOMAN HAS A
RIDICULOUS
VOICE.

WOMAN
OK lovely, thanks
for coming. Could
you all move in a
bit, all move in. So
as you can hear me.
Good. Good. Welcome
to the birthplace and indeed, deathplace
of Alexander Pope the famous poet from
the Olden days. Lovely. Now first off a

few myths to clear up. Number one,
Alexander Pope was not, as many think,
Alexander <u>the</u> Pope. He was no
relationship to the Pope even though he
did go to church regularly on occasion.
Also, neither was he, nor was he ever
nor ever shall be any relation to
Alexander the Great, Alexander
Solzhenitzyn or Nicholas and Alexander.
There is, however, speculation that he is
related to the famous poet, from the
olden days Alexander Pope. Now if you'd
all like to come over here, to the bed...

(THEY ALL CROWD OVER)

area, you can see Pope's bed. Where
Pope slept. And sometimes sat. And
sometimes, perhaps, we can only but
guess, stood on, to reach a book off a
high shelf, or to close a troublesome
window.

TOURIST
May I ask exactly which side of the bed
Pope slept?

WOMAN
Good question, and indeed one that opens
up a can of historical worms. Pope was,
as you may already know, a cripple,
after drinking some infected milk at the
age of 12, and contracting TB of the bone
marrow. This meant that he was a very

ugly twisted little man. He was only 4 ft
6 tall, and he also suffered from asthma,
migraine, heart trouble, eye condition,
urethral stricture, and no sex. He was,
however, charming to old people. So, to
answer your question, sir, hump
permitting, I should imagine he slept
somewhere near the middle of the bed.

TOURIST
Is this where Pope died?

WOMAN
The Pope, or Alexander Pope?

TOURIST
Alexander Pope.

WOMAN
Just testing. Yes indeed. He slipped from
his writing stool at the tender age of 56,
banging his head upon his old friend the
desk, ricocheting off the window,
bouncing along the floor, and finally,
relaxing his bodily muscles and allowing
his juices to trickle out - just here.

**SHE STAMPS HER FOOT - TOURISTS
REACT.**

At least that's my theory.

STONEYBRIDGE - Twin Town

OPENS WITH STONEYBRIDGE PROMOTIONAL VIDEO.

VOICE-OVER
Stoneybridge - Le Jardin d'Ecosse

ANOTHER GENERAL SLIDE
Stoneybridge - L'entree au Nord
Stoneybridge - avec son

SLIDE OF STONEYBRIDGE
Stoneypont.
Stoneybridge - Ou le temps ne marche pas, mais ou il y a beaucoup de temps pour faire choses.

SLIDE OF OLD MAN (CAMPBELL DOCHERTY)
Quelques de nous sont grands

SLIDE OF OLD WOMAN (JOAN DOCHERTY)
Quelque de nous sont vieulles

SLIDE OF 60S COUPLE (GILBERT AND AGNA KENNEDY)
Mais tout le mond habitant en....Stoneybridge.

SLIDE OF TABBY (CAT)

Oh, viens ici Tabby, notre chat. Il n'est
pas sur le parquet, il est en...
Stoneybridge.

GENERAL SLIDE
Stoneybridge...nous ne sommes pas le
twin-town avec quelqu'un...mais nous
voudrons etre twinned avec vous.
Pourquoi? Pour l'argent. Noooooon.
Pour le prestige. Votre
prestige...et...l'argent. Allez
Stoneybridge...allez Paris.

**CUT TO STONEYBRIDGERS
APPLAUDING ENTHUSIASTICALLY.**

ALL
Very good, splendid, marvellous, tres bon....

BRUCE
Well if that doesn't get us twinned with someone...

MAIGRET
Then we'll have to try something else.

WULLY
I'm sure that Vido will do the trick.

EK
Wully, it's Video for Heaven's sake.

WULLY
Well whatever, I'm sure it'll do the trick.

ERCH
Well I must say the French lingo was most impressive. I couldn't understand a word.

MAIGRET
I understood it perfectly. Especially the word Stoneybridge.

MORAY
It's funny that Stoneybridge is the same in French, isn't it?

BOABY
You don't think aiming for Paris is
overstretching ourselves a snatch, no
disrespect Maigret.

MAIGRET
None taken, I'm sure.

ERCH
No, I don't think so. We were described
as the Paris of the East.

BRUCE
No, it was the Partick of the East.

ERCH
Well, whatever it was, it shows we're
being talked about.

EK
Anyway, what do we get out of being
twinned with someone?

MAIGRET
Oh, we get a nice wee sign on the main
road there.

WULLY
Yes, but Maigret what does that lead to?

MAIGRET
Oh, Wully, it leads to the sign at the
other end of the town.

BRUCE
It also brings in work for the sign
maker.

ERCH
Which just happens to be you Bruce.

BRUCE
That's neither here nor there, and I
resent the implication that it is.

WULLY
So who will be making the sign Bruce?

BRUCE
Well, yes, me...about time too...the first
one that'll have been used in 20-odd
years...I've still got a backlot of
"Welcome to the Olympic Village".

BOABY
Still, it's made a beautiful roof for your
cow shed.

ERCH
Yes, it should read..."Welcome to the
Olympic Village - just crap anywhere".

BRUCE
Oh, it does. Well, I wasn't sure about,
you know, foreign types.

EK
Which brings me to my point. Does it

have to be the French? They're a bit of
a messy bunch...as I'm sure Maigret
will bear me out.

MAIGRET
Alec, we don't need to bring that up, do
we?

EK
Fair enough Maigret...but it was you he
got up the stick.

MAIGRET
Just 'cos I never put out for you, Alec.

EK
I never asked....**(TO OTHERS)** don't
listen to her.

BRUCE
Please, please, please...Stoneybridge
Town Council is not interested in
whether Maigret here has seen fit to
engage in carnal congress with wee Alec
here.

WULLY
I am.

EK
Shut up Wully. She certainly never put
out for you.

BRUCE
Gentlemen please. Now, are we all going
to send this video to Paris?

ERCH
Och no...why don't we just twin
ourselves with Muckart...after all, four
of us live there.

BOABY
Yes, we could just tell everyone...save
making the signs...

BRUCE
Can I make the signs anyway, 'cos the
roof of my coop is up the shoot, and the
chickens are soaking?

ALL
Aye... passed.

BRUCE
Right. Eh... any other business?

PAUSE

ERCH
Yes. Maigret, did you put out for Alec
here?

DENZIL - The Visit

DENZIL'S LIVING ROOM. GWYNNEDD IS STANDING AT THE IRONING BOARD, HITTING A PAIR OF DENZIL'S UNDERPANTS WITH A HAMMER. SHE HUMS IN AN UNPLEASANT, TUNELESS WAY. ENTER DENZIL.

DENZIL
Gwynnedd, Gwynnedd! What in Swansea are you doing taking a hammer to my pants?

GWYNNEDD
It are the only way to get them flat, Denzil. The water are too hard.

DENZIL
Too hard? What do you mean, Gwynnedd? The water are too difficult for you? Let me try to explain.

DENZIL PICKS UP A VASE, REMOVES A SOLITARY DAFFODIL FROM IT, AND THROWS THE WATER IN GWYNNEDD'S FACE.

DENZIL
There. Does that make it any clearer?

GWYNNEDD SPITS AND SPLUTTERS.

DENZIL
I really must remember to put some shelves in that space between your ears, Gwynnedd. Oh, that reminds me, by the way. I saw my brother, Illtyd, down at World Of Shelves this afternoon. He are coming round for dinner.

AT THE MENTION OF ILLTYD, GWYNNEDD STARTS SQUEAKING AND MOANING.

GWYNNEDD
Ooooh! Illtyd makes me go weak at the knees.

DENZIL
Yes, well you'd better get your support stockings on, hadn't you?

THE DOORBELL RINGS A LONG SERIES OF BUZZES, RINGS, AND CHIMES, ENDING WITH THE SOUND OF SOMETHING COLLAPSING AND

CRASHING TO THE FLOOR.

DENZIL
That sounds like Illtyd. You'd better let
him in.

**GWYNNEDD, HER SQUEAKING
HITTING EVEN HIGHER PITCHES OF
LONGING, SKIPS TO THE FRONT DOOR.
DENZIL SEEMS IRRITATED BY THIS.**

DENZIL
Ach Y Fi!

**GWYNNEDD RE-ENTERS, WITH
ILLTYD WHO LOOKS LIKE DENZIL IN
MECHANIC'S OVERALLS, AND IS
CARRYING WHAT LOOKS LIKE A
BOUQUET.**

ILLTYD (FLIRTY)
There you are, Gwynnedd. I brought
these for you.

GWYNNEDD
Oh, my favourite! A bunch of sprouts!

ILLTYD
Yes, it are the thought that counts.
Which is why I haven't brought
anything for you, Denzil.

GWYNNEDD
I'll go and get dinner.

**SHE GOES OUT. DENZIL AND ILLTYD
RELAX EXPANSIVELY AT THE DINNER
TABLE.**

DENZIL
Well then Illtyd. How are things down at
Van-U-Like?

ILLTYD
Very good, Denzil. And why haven't you
bought one of my vans? I've got a nice
little Welsh job in at the moment. A
Gwilym Tidy. It would be right up your
street.

DENZIL
The last thing I want up my street are
one of your vans, thank you very much.

ILLTYD
Mr Slightly Thomas bought one last
week, and he are very happy with it, as
a matter of fact.

DENZIL
Yes, well, Mr Slightly Thomas used to be
Mr Completely Thomas, until he bought
one of your vans.

**GWYNNEDD COMES BACK IN,
CARRYING THREE PLATES OF
DINNER ON A TRAY. SHE HAS PUT ON
HER POSH FROCK AND ENOUGH
EYESHADOW AND LIPSTICK TO MAKE**

HER LOOK LIKE A PANDA THAT'S BEEN
SMACKED IN THE MOUTH.

DENZIL
Gwynnedd, have you been attacked or
something?

GWYNNEDD
No, Denzil, I just put some make-up on.

**SHE REMAINS STANDING BEHIND
ILLTYD, BOBBING ABOUT.**

DENZIL
Oh I see, and then you fell down the
stairs. Well, you'd better a sit down then,
hadn't you?

GWYNNEDD
I can't, Denzil. The support stockings are
too poweful.

DENZIL (EXAMINING HIS MEAL)
Gwynnedd, I'm not an expert on cooking,
but this do look very much like a vest
and pair of socks.

GWYNNEDD
Oh, no! Denzil, I must have got mixed up
with the oven and the washing machine
again.

DENZIL
Eeargh! So my dinner will be on the

washing line, will it, Gwynnedd? Don't worry. I'm sure this will be much tastier than the filth what we normally get.

ILLTYD (FORKING A FOLD OF VEST INTO HIS MOUTH)
Delicious, Gwynneddd! And very nourishing too. Vest have got Vitamins Lllllll, Fffffff and Aaaaaaach in it.

DENZIL
Oh, I've had enough of all this Abergavenny.

HE GETS UP SELECTS A SOGGY HAT FROM GWYNNEDD'S PLATE AND PUTS IT ON.

DENZIL
I'm going down to the Club Sboncyn for a nice sensible pint of cheesewater.

HE EXITS.

ILLTYD
Gwynnedd, have you really got support stockings on?

GWYNNEDD
Yes, Illtyd, I have.

ILLTYD (HIGHLY AROUSED)
Gwynnedd, you are one hot chick!

"ABSOLUTELY" - Series Three
Transmission: 10th May – 5th July 1991

Frank Hovis – Taxi
Nice 'n' Nasty
Stoneybridge - Celebrity
The Hurly Burly Bag
Heart Swap
Frank Hovis - Wee-wee
Awkward Seance
The Wellses – Amnesty
Student Letter
Calum – Video
Pizza Fish
Tour Guide
Don & George – Doctors
Frank Hovis – Grease
Calum – Flight
Little Girl – Doctors
Stoney bridge – No Confidence

Designer: Margaret Howat
Director: Alistair Clark
Producer: Alan Nixon

FRANK HOVIS - Taxi

FRANK HOVIS

Good evening, ladies and gentlemen and
welcome to 'On The Lavatory' with Frank
Hovis. I want to share with you an
experience I had a few weeks ago. I had
the misfortune to be taken short in a
public house and the gentlemen's
lavatory just happened to be out of
order. So the landlord said to me,
"Frank, why don't you use the ladies?"
But they wouldn't keep still. So I had to
leave the pub and I rushed out and I
hailed a taxi. "Taxi! Take me to the
lavatory." And away we went. And I can
tell you ladies and gentlemen that by
now there was a titanic struggle going on
in my underpants. I think we were
pretty evenly matched although I reckon
that the poo had the weight advantage.
And I did the best I could, but I am just
flesh and blood and eventually I became
exhausted and I had to, very discreetly,
drop my trousers and, well, I won't go
into details, it's not very nice, but
sufficient to say that I evacuated myself.
Then I pulled my trousers up and I...I
looked around and there was this
monster, lying coiled on the
floor...hissing slightly. I thought for a
moment it might rise up and come at me.
But it didn't do that ... of course, it
didn't. However, I had just crapped in the

back of a taxi. And I wanted to get out.
Apart from anything else the stench was
indescribable. I was very nearly sick. In
fact I was sick. But no, not in the taxi.
No, earlier on in the day. It was a bad
day for me. I...I had the misfortune to be
sick over a tramp. It was a hot meal for
him, I suppose.

Anyway, by now the taxi has stopped
and I get out. And it's not a very nice
thing is it, to do a poo in somebody's
taxi? So I gave him a ten pound note,
well actually it was the fiver I'd wiped
my bottom with, but he didn't know that.

Alright...alright...alright...alright...I
gave him a tip. I said, "Clean out the
back of your cab!"

NICE 'N' NASTY

A POLICE INTERROGATION ROOM, EMPTY EXCEPT FOR A SUSPECT SITTING AT A TABLE. PLAINCLOTHES POLICEMAN 1 ENTERS, VERY CHEERY.

POLICEMAN 1
Rodney, Rodney, Rodney. What are we going to do with you? You can't keep on robbing the banks. It's naughty.

POLICEMAN 2 (ENTERS WITH CUP OF TEA)
Got a nice cup of tea for you, Rodders. There you go. Now what's this I hear? Been robbing banks again, eh? **(TWEAKING THE SUSPECT PLAYFULLY ON THE CHEEK)** You've not to rob banks.

PC 1
So you just sign this nice piece of paper and we'll all go home.

RODNEY
I'm not signing anything until I've seen my solicitor.

PC 2
Won't be a minute Rodders.

PC 1
Enjoy your tea.

(THE POLICEMEN CONFER)

PC 2
What are we doing wrong?

PC 1
One of us is nice.

PC 2
And the other is nicer than that.

PC 1
Yes.

PC 2
That's the system isn't it?

PC 1
It can't be though. Think ... think back
to Hendon. What were we taught.
Remember. Gruff Sergeant Walker.

PC 2
Oh yes, what did he used to say. He used
to say, **(ADOPTS GRUFF VOICE)** "Right
lads..."

PC 1
Oh he did, yes...

PC 2 (GRUFF VOICE)
"Right lads, Interrogation. One of you
has got to be nice, the other must be..."

PC 1
Shy?

PC 2
Was it shy?

PC 1
Well it's worth a try. (THEY EXIT)

PC1 ENTERS AS NICE AS EVER.

PC1
Sorry to disturb you Rodney. Got
everything you need?

RODNEY
Yes.

PC 2
**(HE ENTERS, VERY RELUCTANTLY,
AND SHUFFLES ALONG THE WALL. HE
STARES AT HIS FEET, TWIDDLES THE
BUTTONS ON HIS WAIST-COAT, AND
MUMBLES)**
Rodney, er... did you or did you not rob
the bank?

RODNEY
What?

PC 2
Nothing. Doesn't matter.
**(HE DASHES INTO THE CORNER OF THE
ROOM. PC 1 JOINS HIM)**

PC 1
It's not working is it? God I wish I could
remember. What was it... Nice...

PC 2
And...?

PC 1
Nice and...nice and...

PC 1
Flirtatious?

PC 2
Flirtatious?

PC 1
Yes. Let's try it. You be nice.

PC 2
OK. **(WINKS AT THE SUSPECT)** I'll just
get you another cup of tea Rodders.

PC 1 (COQUETTISHLY)
You lost weight Rodney? Must say you're
looking good.

RODNEY (A LITTLE NERVOUS)
Maybe, why?

PC 1
Oh, you know, nothing.
(SUGGESTIVELY) This seat taken?

RODNEY (VERY NERVOUS)
No.
**(POLICEMEN 1 PLACES THE CHAIR
RIGHT NEXT TO HIM. AS HE SITS
DOWN, LEERING, THE SUSPECT LEANS
BACK IN DREAD)**

PC1
Pass me a biscuit, Rodney?
**(THE SUSPECT QUICKLY OFFERS HIM A
BISCUIT, BUT NOT QUICKLY ENOUGH
TO AVOID PC 1 STROKING HIS FINGERS
AS HE TAKES IT)**

PC 1
Cold hands, eh? Still you know what they
say....
**(PC2 ENTERS, STUMBLES, AND HURLS
A CUP OF TEA ALL OVER THE SUSPECT)**

PC 2
Ooops. Sorry!

PC 1 (RUSHES UP TO PC 2)
What are you doing?

PC 2
Well, flirtatious wasn't working so I
thought I'd try clumsy.
**(BOTH POLICEMEN TURN THEIR BACK
ON THE SUSPECT AND START
WHISPERING. WHEN THEY TURN
ROUND, PC 1 IS HOLDING A UKULELE,
AND THEY BOTH SING)**

BOTH
"Honolulu Baby, oh my oh my, Honolulu
Baby, where d'ya get those eyes"

RODNEY
What is this? Some kind of perverse nice
and nasty routine?

PC 1 & 2
Nasty!

PC 2
Nice ...

PC 1
...and nasty.

PC 2
So obvious.

PC 1
They're opposites of each other, so they
work in tandem.

PC 2
Yes.

PC 1
It's quite clever that, isn't it?

PC 2
So, which one of us is going to be nasty?

PC 1
Well it can't be me. I'm nice by nature.

PC 2
Well, I've never been nasty before
(THEY TURN TO RODNEY)

PC 1
Rodney - unfortunately, neither of us is
in a position to be nasty to you at the
moment, but if you could just bear with
us, there should be somebody nasty
coming along in a minute.

PC 2
Enjoy your tea.

PC 1 AND PC 2 EXIT.

**TIME PASSES. THE SUSPECT IS STILL
ALONE, WHEN INTO THE ROOM
BURSTS A LARGE UNIFORMED
POLICEMAN, DRESSED AND BEHAVING
LIKE A SILENT FILMS VILLAIN,
COMPLETE WITH SWIRLING CAPE AND
TWIRLING MOUSTACHE HE CACKLES
LIKE A PANTOMIME BADDY, AS
LIGHTNING FLASHES AND THUNDER
EXPLODES OUTSIDE. PC 1 FOLLOWS
BEHIND.**

PC VILLAIN
Waaaah Haa Haa Haa Haa Haa Haa Ha! I
have a Court Order to repossess your

smallholding, Rodney. Your possessions
shall be seized and you shall be thrown
onto the streets. Waaah Haa Haa Haa
Haa Haa! You shall be declared bankrupt
and you shall be confined to the
poorhouse. Waaaaah Haa Haaa! Haa Haa
Ha!

PC 1
And then you can have a nice cup of tea.

STONEYBRIDGE - Celebrity

ANOTHER MEETING OF THE STONEYBRIDGE TOWN COUNCIL. GENERAL CHATTER.

BRUCE
Order. Now... Maigret. Thank you. It's now time to select our celebrity to open the Stoneybridge summer jamboree.

ALL
Oh...

BRUCE
So, can I have your suggestions please?

BOABY
Well, can I just say, not wishing in any way to denigrate last year's choice, that I do think that Wully's grandmother was perhaps a wee bit on the elderly side to be cutting the ribbon...

WULLY
Aye, but I mean, she died with a smile on her face...

BOABY
Aye, but we couldnae prise the scissors out her hands...

BRUCE
Objection sustained. Let's set the
celebrity age limit at er ... under 75.

ALL
Aye...

BRUCE
Right, any new suggestions?

MAIGRET
Well, to be perfectly honest, I think we
should discuss a fee.

ERCH
Oh no, Maigret, I don't think they should
have to pay us.

ALL
(MUTTER) No...

MAIGRET
No. We should pay them.

ERCH
No Maigret. They get their photograph in
the local paper - it's very good publicity
for them.

ALL
Aye...

ERCH
It's slightly embarrassing for Wully's
grandmother of course.

WULLY
Right, now, who are we going to ask?

MAIGRET
Well, I don't know if you'll get him now
there's no fee involved, but I think we
should go straight for Tom Cruise.

ALL
Oh.

EK
Tom Cruise? Who's he?

ERCH
Oh, you know...he flies and he looks a
wee bit like Maigret's gerbil.

BOABY
Apparently he's not much taller than
Maigret's gerbil.

WULLY
Well that's no use. We want the folk at the
back to be able to see what's going on.

ALL
Aye...

BRUCE
Well, we could always build him a wee
podum.

WULLY
Or we could stand in a ditch.

ERCH
That aside though, I've always been
rather partial to Tippi Hendren.

WULLY
Be a bit more realistic. What about Sean
Connery?

EK
Oh yes...

BRUCE
Aye...aye. Maigret, haven't you got er...
a contact there...

ALL
Aye Maigret...

MAIGRET
Well, not a contact exactly, no.

WULLY
You told me he once proposed to you.

MAIGRET
No...not exactly...my cousin Moira once
stood three behind him in the queue to
get into the Edinburgh Gaumont in 1954,
if you must know.

ERCH
So you don't think you could just give
him a bell then?
(THEY ALL SNIGGER)

MAIGRET
No. Get on with it.

BOABY
Do you think we should ask Molly Weir?

EK
No. She always says "Yes".

ERCH
Michelle Pfipfiffer's got a nice body.

MAIGRET
Is that a suggestion?

ERCH
No. Just an observation.

BRUCE
Yes. Right I vote Maigret Roneos off a
letter of invitation to them all, and we
re-convene when we've got their replies.

WULLY
Done!
SIX MONTHS LATER. THE SAME PLACE.

MAIGRET
Well. I wrote to a total of 235 celebrities,
and here are their replies. **(SHE HOLDS
UP TWO LETTERS)**

ALL
Oooooh...

MAIGRET
And the fitrst one is from Hollywood.

ALL
Oooooh....

MAIGRET (CLEARING HER THROAT)
Hhmmm. 'Dear Stoneybridge Town
Council, I regret to inform you that
Marilyn Monroe is dead and has been for
a number of years. Yours sincerely...'

ALL
(MUTTER) Oh...

BRUCE
Oh. That's a shame.

MAIGRET
Anyway, here's the other one. 'Dear
Stoneybridge Town Council...'

BRUCE
That's us again.

MAIGRET
Yes. 'Please, please, please can I open
the jamboree this year?'

EK
Who's that from?

MAIGRET
Molly Weir.

BRUCE
Maigret, are you still in touch with that
cousin of yours who stood three behind
Sean Connery at the Edinburgh
Gaumont?

MAIGRET
Don't be ridiculous Bruce. She's not seen
him for 37 years.

BRUCE
No, no. Let's ask <u>her</u> to do it.

ALL
Aye! Good idea... etc.

THE HURLY BURLY BAG

MACGLASHAN IS STANDING OUTSIDE THE OFFICE OF THE LITERARY AGENT, McMINN

MACGLASHAN
Right. Be polite, you want him to buy
your stuff, be courteous, be nice.
Remember the golden rule of selling. Do
not resort to violence. **(RESTRAINING
HIMSELF, HE KNOCKS ON THE DOOR)**

McMINN
Come in **(MACGLASHAN ENTERS THE
AGENT IS SITTING AT A DESK,
FINISHING A PHONE CALL)** Yes, I'll see
you through the week Mr Devie.

MACGLASHAN
All right, Mr MacMahon, how are you
doing?
**McMINN (SPORTING TWO PLASTERS
ON EITHER SIDE OF HIS FOREHEAD)**
Very well considering Mr MacGlashan.

MACGLASHAN
Yes...er... Sorry about that...you know,
you just never know what an artist's
going to do next.

McMINN
Yes. I'm sure Shakespeare was never
done jamming his agent's head in the
filing cabinet. Anyway, I understand
you've got some plays for me.
Tell me about them.

MACGLASHAN
Oh yes, well it's the best stuff I've done
OK. You're going to love this. Right. This
one's called "The Hurly Burly Bag".

McMINN
What's it about?

MACGLASHAN
It's about this bag, OK, called the Hurly
Burly Bag, based on a legend about a
magical bag called...er...

McMINN
The Hurly Burly Bag, aye.

MACGLASHAN
Aye, the Hurly Burly Bag. And if you
find this Hurly Burly Bag and you put
your hand into it, you get special powers
and one wish, and one night this miner's
down near Shorts, you know....

McMINN
Shotts, Bon Accord.

MACGLASHAN
Shotts, Bon Accord aye...out near the
bends there, and it's dark and he finds the
Hurly Burly Bag and he puts his hand
deep into the bag and he gets one wish and
he gets to go on "Sportsnight" and stoat
Jimmy Hill on the head and go "Take that!
You big-chinned English bastard!"

McMINN
Is that it?

MACGLASHAN
No No No. He also gets to shove Elton
Wellsby's face in a food mixer.

McMINN
Well, I don't want to rush to conclusions,
Mr MacGlashan, but it doesn't sound
very dramatic.

MACGLASHAN
It's a comedy.

McMINN
What's your other play called?

MACGLASHAN
"Nip Nap Shite"

McMINN
Well, you've certainly got an eye for a
title. About?

MACGLASHAN
It's a political drama. It's about the SNP.
They put up this candidate called.....

McMINN
MacGlashan?

MACGLASHAN
MacGlashan aye, aye, right...in John
Major's seat, and because he's so
brilliant and Scottish, he wins with a
50,000 majority, and John Major has to
go on television and make this
resignation speech and it goes "Look I'm
really sorry for everything I've done. I
just couldn't help it. I'm just a big
English poof". What do you think?

McMINN
It's pathetic. All your plays are the
same, MacGlashan, they're all about

beating up English people.

MACGLASHAN
Oh they are, are they? What about
"Traveller in Time"?

McMINN
Oh yes, markedly different, a man
invents a time machine, goes back to
1965 and shoots Geoff Hurst.

MACGLASHAN
You're English, aren't you? Forget the
tartan bow tie, you are English. That's
what it is.

McMINN
No, what it is, is you're racist.

MACGLASHAN
Oh, I'm a racist, am I now? Oh really?
**(HE SUDDENLY TURNS AND APPEALS
TO THE CAMERA)** Is that what you
think, that I'm a racist? Well I'm not and
I can prove it. I agree that all men are
alike. Sure yeah: Australians, Tibetans,
Chinese, Argentinians, French, Russians
- all men are alike...except the bloody
English! And I'll tell you what the
difference is: even if Scotland exists for
another 5,000,000 years we would
never, ever, ever, produce someone like
EMLYN HUGHES! And that's the
difference.

HEART SWAP

IN A HOSPITAL WARD, A DOCTOR IS AT THE BEDSIDE OF A NERVOUS MALE PATIENT.

DOCTOR
Well now Mr Tick, as you know your heart's in a terminal condition and we're going to transplant.

MAN
Tell me Doctor, do you know if the donor has accepted Jesus into his heart?

DOCTOR
Ummmm, I'm afraid I don't, no...

MAN
Because I've accepted Jesus into my heart.

DOCTOR
Good. Good. Well I er...I don't think it's going to affect the operation. We can work round Jesus. He's quite a little fella. Ha ha.

MAN
But if you take my heart out then presumably Jesus will go with it?

DOCTOR
Yes.

MAN
And then I'll have a Jesus-less heart and
then I'll have to go through the whole
process of accepting him into my new
heart, and, well, it's quite a lengthy
business.

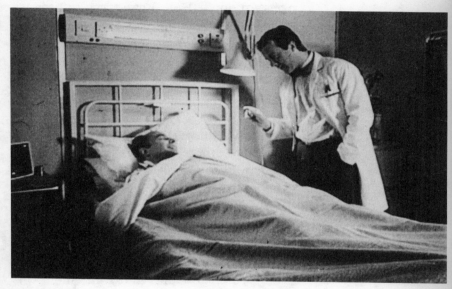

DOCTOR
I'll see what I can do.

MAN
Thank you, Doctor.

DOCTOR (KINDLY)
That's OK.

**(AND AS THE DOCTOR WALKS AWAY, HE
LOOKS INTO THE CAMERA AND MAKES
A "THE MAN'S A LUNATIC FACE".**

FRANK HOVIS - Wee-Wee

Good evening. A bit of advice this week ladies and gentlemen. Don't drink and drive. I don't. Well, I can't really because I smashed my car into a wall just the other night. And as luck would have it, a policeman just happened to be going by, and he came over to me and he said, "Hello...Hello...Hello..." You know the way they do. "I see you've had a little accident". He was absolutely right because I'd just shat myself, as a matter of fact. Easily done. One good cough and you're in all sorts of trouble. And the worst thing about it is the damage that it does to your social life. And I go out quite a lot. Well, I have to really, because I was driven out of the house by...by damp patches, ladies and gentlemen. On the lino. Around the lavatory. The problem is, we've got one of those feminist lavatories where the seat won't stay propped up against the cistern. A sort of...a sort of Venus fly trap. Penis fly trap I suppose. And you know what happens?

You're standing there, passing water, or in my case, urine , and the seat comes down and catches you on the penis. Right on the helmet where it's sensitive. And before you can say "Jack Robinson",

you're up to your ankles in wee-wee. Not
my idea of a cup of tea at all, ladies and
gentlemen. The only thing I could think
of to stop this problem was never to wee-
wee at home. I always go out for a wee-
wee now. Usually with a few friends.
Usually to the pub. We go in, have a wee-
wee. Have a few drinks. Have another
wee-wee. Have a few more drinks. Do
you know, its surprising, because I find
that the more I wee-wee, the more I want
to drink. I don't understand that at all.
And of course, this led to yet another
problem. Because I found that after
about 30 or 40 pints of lager I couldn't
walk. And I was
desperately worried.
But a friend of
mine, he gave me a
bit of advice, he
said, "Frank, try
not drinking". I
thought that
sounded a bit
dangerous, but he
said "no". He said,
"Look, I haven't had
a drink all day and
I can walk now and
I'm going to walk
home". And he did.
And it killed him. I
ran him over on my
way home.

AWKWARD SEANCE

A SEANCE SCENE, WITH A WOMAN WHO IS OBVIOUSLY A MEDIUM, WITH THREE OTHERS SITTING ROUND A TABLE.

WOMAN
Hello...is anybody there? There's somebody there. I sense it. A tall man, grey curly hair. He's holding a rolled up Mackintosh.

KEVIN
It's Dad...it's my father.

WOMAN
He has a message for you.

KEVIN
Yes, what?

WOMAN
It's difficult to make out...

KEVIN
Oh please...try.

WOMAN
Wait...it's coming through...the message is ...**(IN A STRANGE STRANGULATED VOICE)** ..."Hello Kevin".

KEVIN
Yes...?

WOMAN
That's it I think.

KEVIN
That's the entire message? Hello Kevin?

WOMAN
No, wait. There's more.

KEVIN
Yes?

WOMAN (STRANGE VOICE)
Hello Kevin, how's it going?

KEVIN
Fine, fine. How's it going with you?

WOMAN
Oh, you know...not bad.

KEVIN
This is nice.

WOMAN
Yes, indeed. Very nice.

KEVIN
Is that everything?

WOMAN (NORMAL VOICE)
No, he has another message......

KEVIN
Yes?

WOMAN
He says....

KEVIN
Yes?

WOMAN (STRANGE VOICE)
Just to keep going with things the way they are.

KEVIN
And?

WOMAN
That's it... just keep dotting along.

KEVIN
No warnings?

WOMAN
No.

KEVIN
No special things to look out for?

WOMAN (NORMAL VOICE)
Wait, there is something.

KEVIN
Yes?

WOMAN
But he says...it's not really that
important.

KEVIN
So er... what do you do all day?

WOMAN
Nothing much. Watch you mainly.

KEVIN
No point telling you my news then. Huh?

WOMAN
He says he likes Susan.

KEVIN
Yeh...I...I think she's a bit special.

WOMAN
Nice body.

KEVIN
Sorry?

WOMAN
Nice body. Not as tidy as Janet's....but
still not bad. And very good at foreplay.

KEVIN
Don't tell me you watch us when
we're...?

WOMAN
He wouldn't miss it. They all love it.

KEVIN
They?

WOMAN
There's a crowd of them apparently.

KEVIN
Oh well thanks for ruining my sex life.
Nice chatting to you Dad.

WOMAN (STRANGE VOICE)
Bye Kevin. Be seeing you.

THE WELLSES -
Amnesty

**THE WELLSES SITTING ROOM.
JENNIFER WELLS IS TYPING A LETTER
ON A WORD PROCESSOR. PETER WELLS
ENTERS. PROFERRING A BOTTLE OF
SANCERRE (SLIGHTLY CHILLED).**

PETER
How about a little kiss for the new
Assistant V-P?

JENNIFER (ENGROSSED)
In a minute.

PETER SITS DOWN, SOMEWHAT HUFFY.

PETER

Oh, I see, as usual something more
important to do.

JENNIFER

Actually, it's a matter of life and death.
I've just got to get this poor man out of
prison.

PETER

One of your ex-boyfriends, is it? **(HE
SNIGGERS AT HIS OWN JOKE)**

JENNIFER

No, Peter, you know perfectly well who
I'm talking about. Mambazo Mpfuto. We
got his name from Amnesty. He's in
prison, and we promised to write to him
and the government demanding his
freedom.

PETER

OK, let me see it. **(READING OFF THE
THE COMPUTER SCREEN.)**
"Dear Mr Mpfuto. How are you? We are
fine, thank you. It looks like Peter's
going to get his promotion. What sort of
records do you like? Our current
favourites are "Gracelands" by Paul
Simon, and Johnny Clegg and his
Sambucca. I'm glad to say Mummy's
much perkier now. She says "Hello",
although of course I haven't told her
you're coloured, so keep schtum on that

one. Of course, the big news is that we
had five days of glorious sunshine over
the bank holiday - wouldn't raise an
eyebrow in your neck of the woods, but I
tell you, it's a Godsend to us."
Oh, well done, Jennifer. He'll be out by
Monday.

JENNIFER
Oh, don't be so mean, Peter. How would
you feel if you were in his shoes?

PETER
If he's got any.

JENNIFER MAKES A "TUT, TUT" FACE.

PETER
Well, alright. What's he in for, anyway?

**JENNIFER HANDS HIM AMNESTY'S
LEAFLET**

PETER
(READING)
Oh, dear ...

JENNIFER
What is it, Peter?

PETER
He's a member of the ANC!

JENNIFER
Well, it's just a sort of club.

PETER
Oh, play badminton, do they?

JENNIFER
No. They have discussions, and I should
imagine...coffee mornings.

PETER (GETTING HEATED)
Look now, no, listen...listen...I'm not
saying they do...and I'm not saying they
don't...it's just something which, at this
stage in our careers, I don't think we
should be mixed up in.

JENNIFER
OK.

PETER
Get on the phone.

SHE DOES.

JENNIFER
Hello, Amnesty? Jennifer Wells, here.
Yes, there's a bit of a problem with Mr
Mpfuto. Yes. Our pen pal. My husband's
a little bit concerned that he might be a
bit of a villain...no, not at all...

PETER (TAKING PHONE)
Give it here, give it here...

JENNIFER
Just ask for another one....

PETER (TO PHONE)
Peter Wells here. Now, I'm not saying
they've got him bang to rights, but you
must admit there's a bit of a grey area
here ...so, basically, how about a swap?
Who? Rambazo Pampopo. **(TO
JENNIFER)** Rambazo Pampopo?

JENNIFER
Is that a man or a woman?

PETER (TO PHONE)
No - drawing a bit of a blank at this end,
I'm afraid. Oh, he's in the ANC? No,
we're trying to shy away from that
whole area. We don't mind the RAC.

JENNIFER
Try a different crime...

PETER
You don't have anyone in for tax
offences, do you?

JENNIFER
Like Lester Piggott?

PETER
Oh yes...a kind of black Ernest Saunders
would be nice.

JENNIFER

Or a musician would be nice.

PETER (BACK TO PHONE)

Yes, what about a musician?

JENNIFER

Try Errol from Hot Chocolate.

PETER

Oh yes... or Labbi Siffre?

JENNIFER

Michael Jackson?

PETER

Michael Jackson? No, I don't think he's
black any more. **(TO THE PHONE)** Any
of these people been put in priso... Hello?
They've hung up!

JENNIFER

What are we going to do about the letter?

PETER

Just send it to your mother - she'll think
it's a postal order.

STUDENT LETTER

**A FIRST YEAR STUDENT IS SITTING IN
HER ROOM, WRITING A LETTER TO
HER BOYFRIEND.**

Dear Rick. Thanks for your card, letter,
telegram, photo and flowers. They all
arrived on the first day. University is
strange. At times one is gripped with a
unique and delicious sense of
independence, whilst at others one feels
strangely, solipsistically alone, even in
the midst of a crowd. Isn't it ironic. To
feel at once happy, and at once sad, and
to have that Fitzgeraldian, heightened
awareness that one is perhaps
experiencing the best moments of one's
life. Though obviously I'm not, 'cause

you're not here. You're there. And
though you're there, I often feel that
you're here. And wish that you're here.
But you're not. You're there. Anyway,
let's not get too deep. Now for my news.
Well I've already got a major friend. He
helped me carry my mega-trunk up three
flights of stairs to my room on the first
day - boy, did I go red, as Seb later
pointed out. His real name's Sebastian,
but he's really embarrassed about it,
because he's a socialist. Anyway, he's in
the second year, so he's pretty mature
but at times he's completely silly. Eg.,
yesterday we were walking through the
market square, and he went up to a
complete stranger and said 'Smile if you
had sex last night'. We just fell about.

'Humph' I can hear you say, but at
least I haven't gone near anyone druggy.
Seb, who had a bad experience last term
with some Hash Brownies, says he'll
protect me from any serious pushers.
I've told Seb all about you, and he thinks
you sound like a 'great bloke' - his
words, and he's really looking forward to
meeting you. On that subject, I don't
think it's the best idea in the whole wide
world if you come up next weekend. I
think I should settle in a bit longer and
be a big, brave girl. So how about leaving
it till next term? Write soon, but don't
worry if I don't reply. Busy, busy, busy.
Love and hugs. Melanie.

CALUM - Video

**CALUM ENTERS A CROCERS-CUM-
VIDEO SHOP, WITH A CARRIER BAG
FULL OF TAPES.**

CALUM (OFFERING A VIDEO)
Ah...I'm, er, just handing this back.

ASSISTANT
Oh thank you. **(CHECKS HER BOOK)** Ah,
I'm afraid it's a day late.

CALUM
No, it's not.

ASSISTANT
Yes. You borrowed it two days ago.

CALUM
No. It says on the video I could have it
for 48 hours.

ASSISTANT
No sir. The video is called "48 Hours".

CALUM
Oh. I thought that was when it was due
back. Oh, well I think this one might be
late as well then. **(PRODUCES ANOTHER
VIDEO)**

ASSISTANT
What is it?

CALUM
Friday the 13th. I've had to wait two
months for a Friday the 13th.

ASSISTANT
Well sir. Have you got anything else that
might be a little late?

CALUM (PULLING OUT MORE VIDEOS)
"9 1/2 Weeks". "Same Time Next Year"...
which it is, by the way.

ASSISTANT
Thank you. We've been looking for these.

CALUM
And I've also got "About Last Night", er
which like really confused me 'cos like
when is that, you know? If I bring it in

today, is that "about last night?" Is that near
enough for you?

ASSISTANT
Just bring it back anyway, alright. We're also
looking for some other titles. "Forever Yours"?

CALUM
Aye, I kept that.

ASSISTANT
"For Your Eyes Only"?

CALUM
Trust me. No-one else has seen it.

ASSISTANT
"1941"?

CALUM
Don't know how you ever expected to get that
one back.

ASSISTANT
Look. In the circumstances, if you just bring
all these titles back, I won't say another word
about it, alright?

CALUM
Me neither. Right, I'm looking for one other
film.

ASSISTANT
What's it called?

CALUM
Can't remember.

ASSISTANT
Well, who's in it?

CALUM
Oh, it's that guy, the tall guy, with the hair, he's in black and white, well it's grey mostly, if you ask me. But, like, they always say it's black and white.

ASSISTANT
Look I'm sorry. I can't help you.

CALUM
But he plays...he plays a sheriff... and he marries this woman, and he can never remember the time and he's always looking up at the clock...and then there ...there's these people that are after him...and he's...he's going to go and then he's going to stay and then er...everyone else in the town goes out for lunch and then he's on his own and these guys are walking down the street and they are singing "Do not forsake me, oh my Goodness", 'cos of course they couldn't swear in those days, and then he kills them, one by one, and he looks at the clock again and it's one o'clock, so him and his bird go off for lunch like they were going to in the first place.

ASSISTANT
"High Noon".

CALUM
Damn. I've seen it. Have you got anything
with er...James Cagney and...

ASSISTANT
"White Heat"?

CALUM
Sylvester Stallone together, 'cos they're
my favourites. Or Davey Bond. Davey
Bond and 007. "You Only Look Back In
Anger...Twice." That one.

ASSISTANT
Look, I'm busy.

CALUM
I've never heard of it!

ASSISTANT
No, I was saying... Look, I... Oh, you've
never heard of "Look, I'm Busy"?

CALUM
No. Is it good?

ASSISTANT
Is it good! 17 Oscars. Ummm...it's got
ummm...Jimmy Cagney, Sylvester
Stallone, er...Sean Connery...

CALUM
John Wayne?

ASSISTANT
He's there.

CALUM
Laurel and Hardy?

ASSISTANT
Laurel and Hardy.

CALUM
Don't like them.

ASSISTANT
Brief appearance.

CALUM
OK. I'll take it... Where is it?

ASSISTANT
Right...It...it's over there through the
door marked EXIT.

CALUM
Exit?

ASSISTANT
Er...yeah... Extra Interesting Titles.

CALUM
Brilliant.

PIZZA FISH

**A MAN IS SITTING IN A RESTAURANT.
A WAITER APPROACHES**

WAITER
Are you ready to order sir?

MAN
Yes - just a couple of questions. Do you
have any of those very flat fish covered
in different toppings?

WAITER
Sorry?

MAN
You know...a big round fish covered in
cheese and pepperoni.

WAITER
Pizza?

MAN
Yes, the pizzafish.

WAITER
No.

MAN
Oh. Well, do you have any fish at all?

WAITER
Yes sir, we have a wide range of fish.
**THE WAITER POINTS TO THE MENU,
BUT THE MAN IGNORES HIM. THE
MAN POINTS TO THE FISH TANK.
THERE IS ONE LOBSTER IN IT.**

MAN
Is that veal spoken for?

WAITER
Which veal is that?

**MAN (ASTONISHED AT THE WAITER'S
IGNORANCE.)**
The veal. The baby veal in the tank.
What is this? Your first day or
something? HUH!

WAITER
No sir. You can have that veal.

MAN
Right, and how do you prepare the veal?

WAITER (POINTING AT THE LOBSTER)
That veal ... or veal in general?

MAN
Veal. How do you prepare the veal?

WAITER
In breadcrumbs.

MAN
I see. Is the bread fresh?

WAITER
Well, we crumb it daily sir.

MAN
I am not interested in how you prepare
it. Where do you catch it?

WAITER
The bread?

MAN
Yes, the bread. Where did you catch the
bread?

WAITER
Sainsbury's.

MAN
Right, it's freshwater bread, OK. What
about the sauce?

WAITER
It's a caper sauce, sir.

MAN
Right, little ants.

WAITER
Yes sir...little green ants.

MAN
Alright then. I'll have the vealfish, fished
in the freshwater bread in little green
ant sauce.

WAITER (VERY RELUCTANTLY)
Vegetables, sir?

MAN
Oh yes. Tell me is the courgette boned?

WAITER
As far as I know, sir.

MAN
Courgette in that case, thank you.

WAITER
Very good.

MAN
Oh, and a side salad.

WAITER
Green or mixed?

MAN
Kipper or anchovy? I've probably had
enough seafood. I'll have the kipper
salad.

WAITER
The kipper salad? Which is the er....?

MAN
The green one! Ha! Your tip's getting
pretty small laddy.

**A VERY LARGE AND EMBARRASSED
CHEF ENTERS FROM THE KITCHEN TO
ADDRESS THE CUSTOMERS.**

CHEF
Ladies and gentlemen, if I could have
your attention please. I have some
rather bad news for you.

CUSTOMERS (COD DISAPPOINTMENT)
Aww....

CHEF
Unfortunately, we have just run out of
food.

MAN & WAITER
Oh...that is bad news isn't it?

CHEF

Not particularly bad news if you're a
bookshop perhaps, but really quite
disastrous news if you are a restaurant,
which is what this am, I is, we am, is
are, is be. I suppose we could close down
and then instantly re-open as a
bookshop, but, alas, we have run out of
books also.

MAN

You could always re-open as a chef's hat
shop.

CHEF

Do not think for a moment, sir, that I am
ungrateful for your suggestion. But
alas...

**(HE REMOVES HIS CHEF'S HAT TO
REVEAL THAT HIS HEAD, IN FACT, IS
THE SAME SHAPE)**

...no.

TOUR GUIDE -
Etcetera

**THE TOUR GUIDE IS TAKING A GROUP
OF TOURISTS ROUND SOME
CATACOMBS**

GUIDE
And welcome to the official guided tour
of the famous Gatewoods Cemetery. If we
move down here we come to the bit of
the graveyard that reads like a 'Who's
Who' from 'Who's Who', and indeed we
have the first Dr Who buried here. Just
here is the grave of Jonathan Swift, who
suffered from elephantiasis of the
testicle. They grew so large that he had
to wheel them around London in a
wheelbarrow, and his familiar cry of
"Cockles and mussels, alive-alive-o" was
often heard by Nell Gwynn, buried here,
mistress of William of Orange, the
Catholic Protestant. Now, if we move on ,
we come to the grave of George Eliot, the
lady who dressed as a man. Her real
name was T.S. Eliot and her true identity
was discovered one day whilst she was
having a secret bra fitting in a pipe shop
in Berwick Street. Now just here is the
grave of Oscar Wilde, the fat poet, whose
body tragically exploded in Paris, killing
a gravedigger and causing a terrible
pong. Along here are the remains of the

Bronte Sisters, the famous a-capella
singing group of the '60s. They looked
alike, dressed alike and died of a terrible
chesty cough alike.

Passing them, we come to the grave of
John Constable, the village Bobby, who
painted such masterpieces as "The
Haystack" and "The Fighting Demerara".
He stopped painting when he got
promoted to sergeant, but began again as
he became John Singer Sargeant
inventor of the sewing machine. Ah,
now, here's an interesting one. This was
once thought to be the grave of Jack The
Ripper, the man who used to harass
prostitutes by slapping them on the
bottom with a kipper. He is buried with
his son, Nipper, his nail clippers, and his
favourite pair of slippers.

DON & GEORGE - Doctors

GEORGE IS SITTING AT THE TABLE STARING OUT TO SEA. DON IS STANDING ON THE OTHER SIDE OF THE ROOM, LOOKING AT HIS WATCH, AND LEANING AGAINST NOTHING.

DON
5, 4, 3, 2, 1 -
Damn.

GEORGE
What is it Don?

DON
I've just missed
my doctor's
appointment.

GEORGE
Well I could give you a medical. There's a
history of doctoring in my family.

DON
Really?

GEORGE
Oh yes. All of us have been to the
doctor's at one time or another.

DON
So, you could give me a medical then?

GEORGE
I could give you a medical now... Well
come in, take a seat er...Mr er...Mr er...
Mr er...

DON
Thank you...Doctor.

**(DON SITS HIMSELF OPPOSITE
GEORGE)**

GEORGE (TAKING NOTES)
Right. Fine. Name?

DON
Yes thanks.

GEORGE
Say Ah.

DON
Ah.

GEORGE
B?

DON
B

GEORGE
C?

DON
C

GEORGE
D?

DON
D

GEORGE
I think we can skip through this, don't you?

DON
Yes.

GEORGE
Yes. Z?

DON
Z.

GEORGE
So far, so good. Now, can you strip down to your underpants?

DON
Oh yes.

GEORGE
Excellent. You don't have any problems undressing then?

DON
I don't have any problems undressing now.

GEORGE
Heartbeat?

DON
(FEELS HIS HEART. PAUSES) There's
one.

GEORGE
Heartbeat, one. Good. Now, eyesight. Can
you see me doing this? **(STARTS DOING
SILLY WOBBLY DANCE ROUND THE
ROOM)**

DON
Afraid so.

GEORGE
Right, can you see that wall chart over
there?

DON (LOOKING AT EMPTY WALL)
No.

GEORGE
Correct. Eyesight perfect.

DON
I don't need glasses then?

GEORGE
You don't need glasses now. **(THEY BOTH
TURN AND GRIN TRIUMPHANTLY INTO
THE CAMERA)** Right, what height are
you?

DON
5'11".

GEORGE
Yes. In your socks?

DON
5'10"

GEORGE
And with a proper hairstyle?

DON
5'8" and a quarter.

GEORGE
Now, do you smoke?

DON
No.

GEORGE
How many a day?

DON
40.

GEORGE
Right. You don't smoke 40 a day. Do you exercise regularly?

DON
Oh yes. I always go for a swim on my birthday.

GEORGE
When's that?

DON
February 29th.

GEORGE
So you swim regularly, once every four
years. Excellent. How old are you?

DON
Seven and a half.

**GEORGE (STANDS UP AND CLUTCHES
HIS OWN GROIN)**
Cough.

DON
(COUGHS)

GEORGE
Oh dear, we'll have to give you
something for that. OK. **(STICKING OUT
HIS WRIST)**
Can you feel that?

**DON (HOLDING GEORGE'S WRIST LIKE
A DOCTOR)**
Yes.

GEORGE (VERY ANXIOUS)
How am I?

DON
You're fine.

GEORGE
How do you feel?

DON
Very well.

GEORGE
Well that's a good sign.
**(GEORGE CROSSES BEHIND DON AND
REACHES OVER TO GRAB A NIPPLE)**
Does this hurt?

DON
Yes.

GEORGE (TWISTING HARDER)
What about this?

DON
Yes!

GEORGE (NOW STRANGLING DON)
And this?

DON
Yes!

GEORGE
Good. I must remember that. Diet?

DON
I beg your pardon.

GEORGE
Have you ever thought about going on a diet?

DON
Have you ever thought about wearing a wig?

GEORGE
Have you ever thought about tidying up round here once in a while?

DON
Have you ever thought about unpac .....

GEORGE
End of examination.

DON
What's the verdict doctor?

GEORGE
I have some very bad news. We're both still alive.

BOTH CRY

FRANK HOVIS - Greece

Good evening, ladies and gentlemen.

Well as you can see, I've just come back from a little holiday in the Mediterranean. Had a couple of weeks on a little Greek island called Anus... Anus in the Sun. I thought it was quite well named actually because all the sewage from all the Mediterranean came out into the sea just there. They had big signs up on the beach for swimmers saying, "Now Wash Your Hands!". If you wanted a tan you went for a swim. It was horrible. But it didn't stop us having a good time. By Christ no! There was a few of us went and I remember on the first night this one bloke got absolutely paralytic, ladies and gentlemen. Absolutely bloody legless he was. At the end of the evening we had to carry him up the stairs, get him undressed, get his teeth out,... I think we should have got him back to his room as well, but you can't think of everything can you? But the next morning he was furious. He was absolutely furious. Because, apparently he didn't have false teeth. He does now, obviously.

Actually I had a strange experience there myself. I woke up one morning and I thought, "That's funny, I don't remember going to sleep wearing tartan pyjamas", and then I realised, ladies and gentlemen, that I'd been sick over my suit during the course of the night. I blamed the food. I didn't like the food at all. It was the grease. The grease. The grease. There wasn't enough of it in my opinion. I like food that squeaks when you stick your fork into it. But enough about me, ladies and gentlemen. What about you? Well, since last week's show, several people have written to me. But that's neither here nor there.

(HE REACHES FOR THE TOILET PAPER, BUT SEES THERE'S NONE THERE AND WITH A SIGH, HE UNDOES HIS TIE...)

CALUM - Flight

CALUM AT HOME ON THE PHONE TO AN AIRLINE SALES OFFICE

REP
Hello, North-South Airlines, can I help you?

CALUM
I'd like to book a flight please.

REP
Where are you going sir?

CALUM
I'm going to see Gavin, my mate.

REP
Mmmm. Where does Gavin live, sir?

CALUM
47 Manor Park, top bell.

REP
Which town, sir?

CALUM
Oh sorry...er...New York.

REP
Oh I think that can be arranged, sir.

CALUM
Brilliant. When's the flight?

REP
We have a flight leaving every day sir.

CALUM
Oh, one'll do me. What about Saturday?

REP
Yes, we have a flight sir. It leaves
London Heathrow at 1100 hours, arrives
New York JFK at 1300 hours.

CALUM
Brilliant! Only two hours and I'm there
in time for lunch. I'll take it.

REP
There is a time difference, sir.

CALUM
Oh, so what time do they have lunch in
New York?

REP
Lunchtime.

CALUM
No, that's exactly the same as me.
Perfect.

REP
No...er...they're five hours behind us sir.
The flight takes seven hours. Effectively
you land at 6 o'clock. Gaining five hours.

CALUM
Does that cost extra?

REP
What?

CALUM
Those extra five hours.

REP
No. They're free.

CALUM
I'll take them.

REP
Right. One seat. Now your booking
reference, if you'd like to take this down,

is R for Romeo, U for Uniform, D for
Delta, 8....

CALUM
For?

REP
Eight.

CALUM
Eight for eight.

REP
Q for Quebec and I for India. OK sir?

CALUM
OK.

REP
And your name sir?

CALUM
Gilhooley.

REP
Can you spell that sir?

CALUM
Aye.

REP
No. To me!

CALUM
Oh sorry. Well, it's Gilhooley. That's G
for...G for gnome.

REP
Gnome!

CALUM
Gnome! That's...G for gnome like I said.
N for Gnome. O for nothing. M for
medicine and E for Edicine. Gnome!

REP
G!

CALUM
G. Then it's I, er... as in me, as in
medicine and Edicine, as opposed to I as
in Edicine, Yedicine and Edicine. Which is
coming later.

REP
I.

CALUM
Aye.

REP
Double I.

CALUM
No. L.

REP
No L.

CALUM (GAZING OUT THE WINDOW)
No L for ... L for ...er... look at the size
of that Honda! I didn't think they made
1000cc's. Obviously they make 1000cc's
now. I think I'll get a Honda the next
time.

REP
L!

CALUM
L. Then H for...oh I cannae think of
anything for H that...that bike put me
right off! H for...

REP
Honda?

CALUM
I know it's a beauty. H for...

REP
Honda!

CALUM
Of course. H for Henry Honda. I'm
enjoying this. O for nothing. O for...

REP
Nothing.

CALUM
What?

REP
Nothing.

CALUM
Sorry, I thought you said something.

CALUM
O for ...O for Oh! as in Gosh! then L for -
oh, we've done that, yeah - look at the
size of that Honda! I didn't think they
made 1000cc's. They obviously make
1000cc's now, I think I'll get a Honda the
next time.

REP
L!

CALUM
L. Then E for Edicine and Y for ... York.
York, of course, York!

REP
York. Yes!

CALUM
Gavin lives in York, not New York. **(HE
HANGS UP.)**York. I knew there was
something bugging me.

LITTLE GIRL - Doctors

Yes, I do know what happens when you go to the Doctors. First of all you do go into a room where there are lots of mummies and babies, and they are crying and they have got crusty dribble coming out of their noses. And they do smell like underneath your Dad's arms. And there is a old man in the corner wif no teeth and black dots on his nose, and you must not ask your mum why his eyes are looking in different ways. **(SHE GOES CROSS-EYED)** Then the nurse comes out of the window like a cuckoo clock, and she is furious, and she says "Go away, you're late. Eat this recipe three times a day".

And the Doctor does wear a special white coat made out of Vim and that is felous when he does the operation, all the food wot you et for lunch does jump out and plop on his coat, and it does go alive and run all over the place singing "We like coffee, we like tea, we like crisps and we like wee". And then the Doctor says to your mum "What does the matter seem to be madam?" and she says "I got a terrible headache" and then he says: "Ha ha! Take your trousers off then". And then your mum does lie down, and the Doctor does put on the

sunglasses and a special hat, like wot
underground diggers wear and he gets a
great big long stick, with oinkment on it,
and he does have a good old poke.

And he says "Mm, isn't it a nice day?"
Then he does take the stick out, and if it
has got a liver on it, then it is OK. But if
it has got a maggot on it, then that
means your mum has got an ants nest
up her bottom, and they will have to get
the Rat Catcher to get it out with the
vacuum cleaner.

Then the Doctor does give your mum a
bandage, and he does put a rubber ring
on her arm and he does pump it to make
her arm susplode. And then he does say
"Yes you have got enough blood" and he
puts it in a bottle and he drinks it later.
Then he does put a hosepipe on your
heart to see if your bosons have grown
yet. And that is wot happens at the
Doctors. It is. It's true.

STONEYBRIDGE - No Confidence

THE STONEYBRIDGE COMMITTEE ROOM. MAIGRET AND WULLY, ARE STANDING IN A CORNER, CONSPIRATORIALLY. BRUCE IS ABSENT

MAIGRET
All I'm saying is, I think it's time for a change.

WULLY
But he's only been Chairman for 15 years. He's just finding his feet.

MAIGRET
But I just think it's time for someone
else. Someone smaller, perhaps. Someone
who maybe gives you a lift home after
every meeting.

WULLY
Oh, I see what you're saying.

MAIGRET
See, if I was in charge, I'd probably be in
a position to drop you at your door,
instead of at the end of the road.

WULLY
Right, what do I have to do?

MAIGRET
A vote of no confidence.

WULLY
You're on.

MAIGRET
Ooh, and remember, pick your moment
when he's least expecting it.

WULLY
Give me some credit, Maigret.

**BRUCE ENTERS AND SITS DOWN,
EXCHANGING CHEERY "EVENINGS".**

BRUCE
Aye Aye. Well, good evening everyone.

Nice to see so many...

WULLY (WILDLY)
Vote of no confidence!

BRUCE
What's he talking about?

MAIGRET
It's a vote of no confidence Bruce...
we've got to hear it immediately.

BRUCE (CRACKING)
15 years of service, day in day out, man
and boy...for this! To be cast aside
like...like...like so much...
BRUCE STRUGGLES FOR WORDS.

EK
Cowdung?

BRUCE
I take it you're supporting the motion?

EK
Well...aye...perhaps...maybe I...er...not
very much confidence anyway.

BRUCE
Et tu Erchie?

ERCH (GRINNING)
Et me Brucie.

BRUCE
Boaby, surely not...?

BOABY
Bruce, I am behind you 100 per cent of
the way.

BRUCE
Right. The fight is on. Which of you
Judas's is standing against me?

WULLY
I am not at liberty to disclose that
information, Bruce, but I will say that
I'm her campaign manager.

BRUCE
Maigret? A woman? A woman has never
run Stoneybridge Town Council and
never will.

ERCH
Fancy Frank Allen used to dress up as a
woman.

BRUCE (RISING TO LEAVE)
We shall skate over that shameless
period in our history. The Council is now
in safe hands and shall remain so.
Fifteen more years. Come on Boaby.

BOABY
Aye.

**BRUCE AND BOABY STOP BY THE
DOOR.**

GORDY
By the way Boaby, why were you so
firm in your support?

BOABY
Well I thought we could use my old
campaign sign. **(HE PICKS UP A SIGN
PROCLAIMING "BOAB'S YOUR UNCLE")**
I thought we could just score out the
Boab and put in Bruce.

BRUCE
Oh thanks for your undying support
Boaby. Come on.

**LATER: ON THE STREET. BRUCE IS ON
A SOAPBOX FLANKED BY BOABY WITH
HIS NOW CRUDELY ALTERED SIGN.**

ERCH AND EK ARE LISTENING.

BRUCE
If re-elected I guarantee to make sure
that our Stoneybridge remains exactly
where it is.

EK
Is that it?

BRUCE
No sir. That's not it. The bus stop is also
safe in my hands, position-wise.

ERCH
Oh bugger this Alec, let's go somewhere
else.

**THEY MOVE OFF - THREE FEET TO THE
LEFT WHERE MAIGRET IS STANDING
ON HER SOAPBOX, ATTENDED BY
WULLY.**

MAIGRET (TO WULLY)
Bruce has got a banner...why didn't you
make me a banner?

WULLY
Well Boab's got the only one in the
village.

MAIGRET
Well do something to draw attention to
me then.

ERCH
Excuse me, could you speak up please?
Your manifesto, if you will.

MAIGRET
Oh. When elected I promise to do things.
Things that have not been done before.
New things...

WULLY (DROWNING HER)
Maigret! Maigret! Maigret! In! In! In!
Bruce! Bruce! Bruce! Not in! Not in! Not
in!!

BRUCE (POINTEDLY)
Willy. Willy. Willy. Noted. Noted. Noted.

**LATER: AT THE POLLING BOOTH. ERCH
IS ABOUT TO VOTE, WHEN BRUCE
HANDS HIM A TURKEY WITH A SLIP OF
PAPER ATTACHED TO IT.**

BRUCE
Oh...Erchie...just er... that's your ballot
paper there.

ERCH
All right, yes...

BRUCE
**(NOW HANDING OVER A VERY LONG
STRING OF SAUSAGES WITH A PEN ON
THE END)**
And you'll need something to make your
mark...

ERCH
Oh, a wee pen...

**LATER: THE RESULT IS ANNOUNCED,
WITH WULLY ACTING AS THE
RETURNING OFFICER...**

WULLY

Now owing to the rules of the election,
the candidates themselves are barred
from voting. As are the campaign
managers. So therefore the votes cast in
the election are as follows. Bruce Gilbert
Wendell Aloysius MacGrory. One. Maigret
Marjory Mary Mirabelle MacKenzie. One.
That makes the final count One One. So,
either we sort of keep things as they are,
or we could have another election...?
**(HE LOOKS TO HIS AUDIENCE OF EK
AND ERCH WHO ARE SITTING,
PUFFING CIGARS, AND SMOTHERED
WITH VOTE-LURING BOOTY)**

EK

Another election I think.

ERCH

More campaigning, if you get my
meaning.

SOME "ABSOLUTELY" SONGS

The Journey of Life (Series 1)

Clever (Series 2)

Anthem (Series 3)

THE JOURNEY OF LIFE
SUNG BY SIX REFUGEES FROM THE
SUNDAY EVENING "GOD SLOT".
As we walk through the voyage of life,
As we travel down the path of being,
As we swallow the bitter pill of failure,
As we reap the fruits of success,
That's the journey, the journey of life.

As we swim the ocean of faith,
As we sail the sea of destiny,
As we contemplate the life jacket of
failure,
As we're replanted in the garden of joy,
As we inflate the beachball of deception,
As we enter the rabbit hutch of
compromise,
That's the journey, the journey of life.

As we wear the yellow wellingtons of
gloom,
As we play pitch and putt on the golf
course of hopes,
As we climb up the trees of achievement,
As we hang upside down from the skip of
wistful dreams,
As we fish on the bi-way of broken
hearts,
As we bounce up and down on the
trampoline of doubt,
That's the journey, the journey of life.

MR MUZAK - CLEVER

MR MUZAK IS AT HIS PIANO, SMILING AT THE CAMERA IN AN EXCEEDINGLY SMUG SORT OF WAY. HE STARTS TO PLAY AND SING:

Clever, I'm frightfully clever,
Oh, perspicacious rhymes with veracious,
Clever, I sound really clever,
Because I know pecacious rhymes with
pugnacious,
Malicious, pernicious, suspicious,
You probably don't know what they
mean.

Which makes me...

Clever, so fantastically clever,
I can fit in a hell of a lot of words in
every line,
Big words, incredibly big words,
And some of them are really huge,
Ostentatious, rapacious, fugacious,
Palacious, Loquacious, Annunciacious,
You probably don't know,
You probably don't know,
You probably don't know what they
mean.

ANTHEM

A SONG FOR ROCK STARS WHO TELL IT LIKE IT IS

We must stop all this killing now,
All this senseless violence, it must cease,
Life is far too much important
So stop this killing, keep the peace.

All you politicians please tread lightly.
All you world leaders, watch your step.
One false move wrong, the planet pays
the price.
Please remember, Jesus Christ.

Our time is running out, consult your
evolutionary watch.
You will see we're approaching midnight,
The planet's yawning, in the fading light.
We must stop this dream becoming a
night....mare.

Black and white come together,
Yellow and brown, you must unite,
Then black and white must co-exist with
yellow and brown,
Then black and white and yellow and
brown and red...join our global rainbow.

And fight
This problem...
and not each other.

All you preachers, all you teachers,
All you outreachers, all you creatures,
All you speechers with your features,
All you followers of Nietzsche's,
...we'd like to meetcher.

And fight.
This problem...
and not each other.

(BUSK IT FROM HERE)

Yes, so you'd better watch it
And don't do those things any more.
You'd better watch...what you're eating,
OK?
No more...no nonsense...or any
shenanigans,
None of those things should...happen...
Again...like....